Palgrave Insights into Apocalypse Economics

Series Editor
Richard Westra
Graduate School of Law
Nagoya University
Nagoya-shi, Aichi, Japan

This series is set to become the lodestone for critical Marxist and related Left scholarship on the raft of apocalyptic tendencies enveloping the global economy and society. Its working premise is that neoliberal policies from the 1980s not only failed to rejuvenate capitalist prosperity lost with the demise of the post-Second World War 'golden age' economy but in fact have generated a widening spectrum of pathologies that threaten humanity itself. At the most fundamental level the series cultivates state of the art critical political economic analysis of the crises, recessionary, deflationary and austerity conditions that have beset the world economy since the global meltdown of 2008–2009. However, though centered on work that critically explores global propensities for devastating financial convulsions, ever-widening inequalities and economic marginalisation due to information technologies, robotised production and low wage outsourcing, it seeks to draw on exacerbating factors such as climate change and global environmental despoliation, corrupted food systems and land-grabbing, rampant militarism, cyber crime and terrorism, all together which defy mainstream economics and conventional political policy solutions.

For critical Marxist and related Left scholars the series offers a non-sectarian outlet for academic work that is hard-hitting, inter/trans-disciplinary and multiperspectival. Its readership draws in academics, researchers, students, progressive governmental and non-governmental actors and the academically-informed public.

More information about this series at
http://www.palgrave.com/gp/series/15867

Stavros Tombazos

Global Crisis and Reproduction of Capital

palgrave
macmillan

Stavros Tombazos
University of Cyprus
Nicosia, Cyprus

ISSN 2523-8108 ISSN 2523-8116 (electronic)
Palgrave Insights into Apocalypse Economics
ISBN 978-3-030-05724-4 ISBN 978-3-030-05725-1 (eBook)
https://doi.org/10.1007/978-3-030-05725-1

Library of Congress Control Number: 2018965608

Cover illustration: Dina Belenko / Alamy Stock Photo

This Palgrave Pivot imprint is published by the registered company Springer Nature Switzerland AG
The registered company address is: Gewerbestrasse 11, 6330 Cham, Switzerland

In memory of Ernest Mandel

CONTENTS

LIST OF FIGURES

CHAPTER 1

Introduction

Abstract From the early 1980s, the rate of profit recovers, but the rate of accumulation does not track the recovery in profitability. The ratio Surplus Value/Accumulation grows. An ever greater share of surplus value takes the form of money capital and, through credit, is directed to consumption. Marx's schemas of reproduction are modified to show the increasing importance of private debt in the process of realisation of value. Financial derivatives permitted the creation of an enormous volume of fictitious capital alongside an unsustainable debt. The ongoing crisis is not only "financial", but it is also the crisis of the neoliberal regime of accumulation. Economic policies prevented the collapse of the financial system and saved the euro, but they did not lead to an exit from the crisis.

Keywords Ratio Surplus Value/Accumulation • Divergence of rate of profit and rate of accumulation • Financial derivatives • Rhythm of realisation of value • Marx's schemas of reproduction

The global capitalist crisis that broke out in 2007–2008 in the United States (USA) and spread throughout the world, especially in the developed economies, is not only a crisis of the banks and the financial sector. It is a profound structural crisis of capitalism.

More precisely, it is the crisis of neoliberal capitalism. Capitalism never exists in general and abstract terms, but always in specific and concrete

© The Author(s) 2019
S. Tombazos, *Global Crisis and Reproduction of Capital*, Palgrave Insights into Apocalypse Economics,
https://doi.org/10.1007/978-3-030-05725-1_1

manner, that is, in a historical context. The general and diachronic laws of capitalism always manifest themselves through policies and regulations that are historically volatile and subject to change, which, therefore, allows for the periodisation of the capitalist era. "Neoliberalism" refers to the latest regulatory framework imposed gradually since the early 1980s. Even if the neoliberal "dogma" is based on the assumption that the "markets can regulate themselves", the neoliberal regulatory framework exists ("no regulation" means "a different kind of regulation") and is very different from the Keynesian framework, which prevailed in the initial post-war period.

Under the term "crisis", Marxists understand both the "periodic crises" that are a common phenomenon that occurs at relatively regular intervals, and the "structural crises". Many authors identify the "structural crisis" with the "long-term waves of economic contraction" (low investment and GDP growth rates), during which recovery and growth periods are weaker and periodic recessions more acute (Mandel, 1995).

Marx himself dealt only with periodic crises, since the discussion on long-term economic waves, which presupposes a relatively long capitalist history, began after Marx's death. Marx analyses crises in the context of the "industrial cycle" (the short-term cycle) of his era—that is the cycle that Joseph Schumpeter called the "Juglar Cycle"—in contrast to the long-term cycle or the "Kondratieff Cycle". Marx has in mind a ten-year industrial cycle in which fixed capital investment is in some years much more intensive than in other years, with the result that economic activity fluctuates strongly during the cycle.

Essentially, he uses class struggle to explain the various phases of the cycle. Very briefly, in the period of recovery from the periodic crisis, because of the low level of wages, which has a positive effect on the rate of profit, firms tend to invest in particular in circulating capital and absorb some of the "overpopulation". The reduction of the latter stimulates demand. At the same time, however, it increases the bargaining power of the workers and leads to the replacement of part of the variable part of circulating capital with fixed capital, and the replacement of old fixed capital with new fixed capital. This is the reason why, according to Marx, the duration of the industrial cycle is related to the rotation time of fixed capital: Fixed capital is replaced because of its "moral depreciation", long before it is physically exhausted.

The large fixed capital investment leads to a high economic growth and ultimately to "economic overheating", that is to overproduction of commodity values, which undermines growth. The resulting fall in the rate of profit leads to the periodic crisis and the increase of unemployment. The latter undermines wages and increases the profitability of capital. Thus, the industrial cycle begins from the start. In short, class struggle, through its impact on the rate of profit, punctuates the industrial cycle characterised by different stages: crisis, recovery, overheating, and so forth (Marx, 1976).

Our interpretation of the crisis is founded on the theoretical premises provided by Karl Marx. Although Marx did not deal with structural crisis (or long-term waves of contraction) and one does not find in his work a systematic presentation of a theory of crisis, his critique of political economy, that is the very theory of value and capital as expounded in the three volumes of *Capital*, is a valuable tool in understanding both periodic and structural crises, including the current global crisis.

More specifically, we will show that the first four chapters of the second volume of *Capital* (Marx, 1992) analysing "industrial capital", the chapters of the same volume analysing the "reproduction schemas of capital", as well as the analysis of the relationship between "industrial capital" and "money capital", developed in some chapters of the third volume, are indispensable for understanding the current crisis.

In the Marxist debate on the crisis, reference to the downward trend in the rate of profit and the argument over whether or not there has been a decrease or an increase in the rate of profit since 1980 obscures a consideration that has not received due attention: The rate of profit diverges from the rate of capital accumulation. That is to say, the same rate of accumulation of fixed capital requires a higher rate of profit, or for the same rate of profit the rate of accumulation is lower (Husson, 2008, 2010).

This divergence, which is confirmed by the upward trend in the ratio of Surplus Value/Net Investment in fixed capital or the ratio Surplus Value/Accumulation, is, we argue, key to understanding the reproduction schema of capital in the neoliberal era, the role of money capital within it and, ultimately, the crisis as such.

Though we believe (like many other Marxist scholars) that the rate of profit has been increasing during the neoliberal period, the shift of attention from the rate of profit to the above-mentioned divergence permits to avoid a very technical and complex discussion about the calculation of the value of fixed capital stock, which is the key issue in the controversial discussion about the evolution of the rate of profit since the early 1980s. By following the tracks of surplus value, it is possible to present the neoliberal schema of reproduction and its immanent inconsistencies that led to the crisis.

This shift of attention from the rate of profit (analysed in the third volume of *Capital*) to the upward trend in the ratio Surplus Value/Net Investment in fixed capital requires particular attention to the second volume of *Capital*, which seems to be forgotten in many Marxist interpretations of the present crisis.

Particular attention is also placed on money capital, not as one of the three industrial capital circuits developed in the second volume, but as a seemingly autonomous entity (which Marx develops in the third volume of *Capital*) and the way it is conjoined with productive capital (Marx, 1991) during the neoliberal era. Money capital is an essential part of the neoliberal reproduction schema and not just a parasitic organism that undermines the so-called real economy. The role of money capital has been decisive both in the recovery of the rate of exploitation since 1980 and in respect to the rhythm of value realisation.

This book contains six chapters, including the first and the last chapters, "Introduction" and "Conclusion", respectively. In the second chapter, "Profitability, Accumulation and Industrial Capital", official statistical data are provided, indicating that labour productivity has been increasing at a faster pace than real wages, which is tantamount to a growth in labour exploitation. As a result of the increase in labour exploitation, the rate of profit recovers. However, the rate of accumulation of fixed capital does not track the recovery in the rate of profit. Investment in fixed capital proves to be less sensitive to the increase in profitability than in the past, thus creating a gap between the curve of the profit rate and the curve of the accumulation rate. GDP growth, following the rate of accumulation, lags behind the rate of growth in the "golden" post-war period.

Because the official methodology to estimate the value of fixed capital stock is controversial and can have a strong impact on the calculation of the rate of profit according to some authors, we present the ratio of Surplus Value (for surplus value we use a comparable concept available in official statistics: the net operating surplus, total economy) to accumulation (net investment in fixed capital). This reveals a strong upward trend. This ratio confirms the divergence between the rate of profit and the rate of accumulation.

Through the presentation of statistical data, an initial theoretical issue arises. Is it possible for the rate of profit to have been recovering since 1980 and yet still the capitalist economy to have entered one of the most profound crises in capitalist history? Who has stipulated that all major crises of necessity arise from a fall in the rate of profit? Certainly not Marx, whose theory of crises is not mono-causal. The fall in the profit rate may equally be the result and not the cause of the crisis.

The very concept of capital refers to an articulation of economic rhythms, more specifically of three fundamental rhythms. In the first four chapters of the second volume of *Capital*, Marx presents the three circuits of industrial capital: the circuit of money capital, the circuit of productive capital and the circuit of commodity capital. As we have shown in greater detail elsewhere (Tombazos, 2014), the first pertains to the rhythm of valorisation, the second to the rhythm of accumulation and the third to the rhythm of realisation of value. Capitalist growth presupposes a relative compatibility between these three rhythms, while economic crises arise due to the excessive divergence of one of these rhythms in relation to the others.

Every economic crisis can be described as an "organic arrhythmia" of the system. The crisis of the 1970s arose from a slowdown in the rhythm of valorisation of value (fall of profitability), while the current crisis stems from a deceleration in the rhythm of realisation of value. Although the cause of the crisis was different in these two cases, the resultant outcome was a systemic "arrhythmia" of such proportions that it almost immediately caused a severe recession and a long-term effect on GDP growth.

From the analysis of the statistical data also arises a practical consideration: Since surplus value (or "industrial profit") is decreasingly invested in fixed capital, where is it going? In other words, how can the divergence of the rate of profit and the rate of accumulation be explained?

The third chapter is entitled "Private Consumption, Wage Share in GDP and Reproduction Schemas". During the neoliberal period, private consumption and adjusted wage share in GDP deviate. In the European Union of the first 15 member states (EU-15), there is a significant fall in wage share compared to private consumption, while in the USA we have a small fall in the wage share and a significant increase in private consumption in GDP. In Japan, the wage share in GDP is significantly reduced, while private consumption grew. In all three cases the ratio of Private Consumption/Wage Share is increasing.

Looking at the evolution of household debt and savings since the mid-1990s, we find that until the crisis broke out in the USA, there was a large increase in household debt and a reduction in savings (in terms of disposable income percentage), while in the EU-15, there was a small decrease in savings and a large increase in household debt. Only in Japan, there is a simultaneous decrease in household savings and debt.

These empirical observations allow us to conclude that part of the surplus value not invested in fixed capital ended up in the consumption by working-class households who borrowed to consume, thus increasing their debt. The fact that household debt does not increase during the period under review in Japan simply means that part of the surplus value produced there is transferred to other countries, particularly to the USA. Countries with significant export surpluses such as Japan are less dependent on their domestic market than countries whose foreign trade is in balance or in deficit. This is the reason why in Germany, as in Japan, there is no increase in household debt during the period under review. Part of the surplus value produced there was transferred to other European states, particularly to states of the southern Euro area. This explains why Greece, for example, showed very high rates of GDP growth in the 2000s, before the onset of the crisis.

In this chapter, we present and interpret the schemas of simple and expanded reproduction in Marx. As we have shown in detail elsewhere (Tombazos, 2014), these schemas do not intend to indicate that the system will crash after a number of reproduction cycles, nor to show that the system can function without major crisis in the long run (Mandel, 1992). Starting from the realisation process of value, that is the commodity capital circuit, the conditions of equilibrium are determined, which allow for a relatively smooth reproduction of social capital.

Then we develop Marx's schema of extended reproduction by introducing into this the borrowing of workers. In other words, part of the overall surplus value is transferred to workers in the form of loans consumed by the latter.

The modified schema of extended reproduction shows that consumption, investment and production are at a first stage balanced at a higher level: Borrowing stimulates consumption, which has a positive effect on investment and employment, thus leading to greater production.

However, this reproduction schema is structurally unstable and from the outset has an expiration date: The borrowed amounts do not increase only because of the surplus value borrowed, but also due to the interest that accrues from cycle to cycle. Worker household debt service is continuously rising as a share of wages.

Such an unbalanced reproduction schema exhausts its absolute horizon as soon as part of disposable wages shrinks to such an extent that the reproduction of labour power is no longer in tune with debt servicing. It collapses, however, before exhausting its absolute time horizon, once the so-called markets begin to doubt whether the accumulated rights on future wages will be redeemed. Thus, the economic crisis manifests itself initially in its financial dimension, as an accumulation of unsustainable private debts.

The financial system of the neoliberal period has allowed the massive "transfer" of future demand by wage earners in the present time through rising debt, whose servicing has increasingly undermined the disposable part of their wages for consumption.

As we have already mentioned, the accumulation rate does not track the recovery in the profit rate to the extent that it did in the past. However, easy lending stimulated the accumulation rate that would otherwise have been even lower. In other words, money capital has created a huge bubble bursting in 2008, but without which economic growth rates would have been much lower before the crisis.

A further question arises: Why was money capital loaned as easily as it was, without requiring credible collateral from the borrowers?

The fourth chapter is entitled "Money Capital, Fictitious Capital and 'Toxic Capital'". In the context of the neoliberal deregulation of the financial system, investment banks have been able to produce financial derivatives traded on the markets. More specifically, financial derivatives have resulted from the merger of a number of loans and the issue and sale of various securities such as Mortgage-Backed Securities (MBS), Collateralized Debt Obligations (CDO) and Asset-Backed Securities (ABS). In this way, the risk of non-performing loans spread globally in a myriad of investors and portfolios, and was thus considered reasonable. From a system where the granting of a loan meant the assumption of the underlying risk, we move to a system that ostensibly decouples the loan from that risk through its sale in the form of a financial derivative product. The actual quality of the loans was increasingly of less interest to the bankers, while their quantity interested them more and more.

It was assumed that the creation of financial derivative products was a form of financial risk management. Mixing multiple loans into a financial derivative makes the non-servicing of one of the loans less damaging, and hence less of a risk for the creditor. In addition, the creditor may choose to shift the risk by selling the financial derivative. The investment bank grants loans (or purchases loans from the original lender) to turn them into financial derivatives. The hedge funds and other institutional investors who buy these securities sell them to others in their original form or in the form of new financial derivatives (backed by the former), and so on. But this continuous shift of risk to the Generalised Other, which increases the opacity of the financial system, rather than rational risk management, transforms it from individual to social, from private to systemic, from local to national and global. The Generalised Other is all of us, the global system.

The financial crisis first broke out in the USA in the field of financial derivatives on real estate, but it spread very soon to all the sectors of financial derivatives, including ABSs for consumption loans and CDSs (Credit Default Swap) insuring the lender for the loans it granted. The crisis spread from the USA to the UK, and then to the continental Europe and the rest of the developed world.

In order to better understand how the financial system is conjoined with exploitative practices, how it is an organic part of the neoliberal reproduction schema, Marx's analysis of money capital is quite useful. Money capital in Marx is part of industrial capital, not an independent entity. In order for the lender's money (m) to "generate" interest, it must be transferred to the industrial capitalist who will invest it productively together with his own capital in monetary form. In other words, m is only part of the total money (M) in the industrial capital circuits. And interest is only part of the industrial profit.

The same applies to the owner of money buying shares from the industrialist. He gives the industrialist money against a title of ownership over the total industrial capital, from which he requires a share of the total profit: a dividend. This, like interest, is only part of the industrial profit. In Marx, industrial profit includes all the subdivisions of surplus value, all of its "faces": profit remaining in the business after interest and dividend payments (profit of enterprise), interest and dividend.

Marx calls fictitious capital every capital that has a "double life". The industrialist converts into productive capital his own money together with the loan. The lender records in his own "book of accounts" as assets the loan he has extended. This, however, does not exist twice: Once as part of the total money invested (M) and another time independently of it, which does not prevent the lender's assets (when composed of direct borrowing, i.e. shares, and when converted into a financial derivative) to fictitiously expand in the secondary markets, depending on the movement of the "markets", beyond the real value to which they correspond. This "expansion" of value, fictitious capital to the power of two, can be called "toxic capital".

By analogy, the share of public debt that cannot be serviced and is written off (like in Greece in 2012) or the share of the non-performing consumer loans written off corresponds to "toxic values".

Money capital, as a seemingly autonomous entity, does not produce value. Its "profit" arises as interest and dividend from industrial profit for productively invested loans, as interest on taxes levied by the state to service the public debt and as interest from wages for consumer loans to workers. Money capital corresponds to a real value that is either productively invested or consumed privately, but which can expand fictitiously, thus creating a "toxic value" that can have a very serious impact on the real economy.

In the fifth chapter, "Economic Policies and Economic Perspectives", we argue that the volume of this "toxic value" is not given in advance. It is the object of social conflict. The economic policies implemented, prevented to a large extent the depreciation of this "toxic capital".

The central banks of the developed countries performed an unprecedented monetary experiment in economic history. They have thrown into the economy an astronomical amount of many thousands of billions of dollars, reflected in the increase of their assets. Only the three strongest central banks in the developed world, Federal Reserve (Fed), European Central Bank (ECB) and the Bank of Japan, increased their assets from around 3 trillion to 13 trillion, between 2007 and 2017, mainly by buying sovereign debt, but also other securities.

This unprecedented "quantitative easing", by artificially increasing the demand for assets of all types (government debt, financial derivatives, stocks, etc.), kept the price of securities high. Central banks buying public debt securities in secondary or primary markets keep securities prices at high levels, thus preventing the depreciation of their value. An alternative to these quantitative easing practices would be the "haircut" of public debt.

Monetary policy has prevented the collapse of the financial system and in Europe has saved the euro, but has not led to an exit from the crisis. Looking at the official statistical data after the great recession of 2009, we find that the profit rate recovers and surpasses the pre-crisis levels. However, the divergence of the profit rate and the accumulation rate, as well the Surplus Value/Accumulation ratio, is increasing everywhere. Fixed capital investment lags far behind pre-crisis levels. Never in the post-war era was the rhythm of accumulation so slow. The tighter supervision of banks and the stabilisation of the household debt or its decrease in some cases slowed the rhythm of capital accumulation. GDP is growing at a much slower pace than in the pre-crisis period. The most worrying, still, is that labour productivity is growing at an unprecedentedly slow pace in all three major poles of the developed world. Its annual growth rate is around 0.5% per year.

The main pillar of monetary policy was zero or even negative real interest rates by central banks, but these have a number of "side effects" that require central banks to revise it. This policy undermines the traditional banking system, which is based on the conversion of deposits into loans, thus creating incentives to increase deposits. Instead, some banks have already begun to discourage deposits by treating them as "cost".

It also undermines pension funds by lowering the real interest rates on government securities, which in many cases have gone into negative territory (pension funds are forced through legislation to invest a share of their assets in public securities). It creates new bubbles in the real estate and stock markets.

The central banks themselves recognize the need to return to monetary "normality". However, moving from the state of an unprecedentedly prolonged monetary "emergency", which is now prevalent, to a state of normality is not an easy task. It would also adversely affect fiscal policies because it would lead to higher interest rates on public debt. The fact that the transition to less expansive monetary policies could have a very serious impact on economic activity is also recognised by the central banks themselves.

The crisis in Greece, the other southern European countries and Ireland reflects the problems of the Eurozone's architecture. The euro is a common currency which exposes economies of different levels of development to "pure" competition, without an adequate political system. The political integration of Eurozone countries is far behind their economic integration. If one wants to fix permanently the exchange rate of national currencies in a monetary union, it does not merely suffice to abolish the national currencies. One must also develop policies and mechanisms that would make the new currency functional and sustainable.

The crisis in Greece, the other southern European countries and Ireland is interpreted as a crisis of Eurozone architecture. The austerity policies in southern Europe during the last years change, in the long-term, the balance of power between European countries and establish conditions that no longer allow the return to growth rates of the initial euro period in the southern European countries and therefore do not favour the convergence of the Eurozone economies.

Since the early 1980s, neoliberal policies transforming the old Keynesian regulatory framework, transformed also the characteristics of the crises: The crisis of the 1970s was due to the fall in the profit rate. The present crisis is due to the structural slowdown in the rhythm of realisation of value in comparison to the rhythm of valorisation of value. The current crisis, in which always lurks the risk of deflation, is the crisis of the neoliberal response to the crisis of the 1970s, in which the risk of inflation prevailed.

Methodologically, we move from the "abstract" to the "concrete", that is, we try to approach reality by introducing gradually in the analysis the difficulties that its understanding raises. This means that in the following chapters, the reasoning does not take into consideration notions like "interest", "dividend", "private debt", "public debt", "financial derivative products" and so forth before these have formally been introduced in their logical place in the reasoning process.

BIBLIOGRAPHY

Husson, M. (2008). *Un pur capitalisme*. Lausanne: Éd. Page deux.

Husson, M., (2010, January). La hausse tendancielle du taux de profit. Retrieved from: http://hussonet.free.fr/tprof9.pdf

Mandel, E. (1992). Introduction. In Marx, K. (1992). *Capital: A Critique of Political Economy*. Volume Two. London, New York: Penguin Books.

Mandel, E. (1995). *Long Waves of Capitalist Development: A Marxist Interpretation*. London, New York: Verso.

Marx, K. (1976). *Capital: A Critique of Political Economy*. Volume One. London, New York: Penguin Books.

Marx, K. (1991). *Capital: A Critique of Political Economy*. Volume Three. London, New York: Penguin Books.

Marx, K. (1992). *Capital: A Critique of Political Economy*. Volume Two. London, New York: Penguin Books.

Tombazos, S. (2014). *Time in Marx. The Categories of Time in Marx's Capital*. Leiden, Boston: Brill Academic Publisher.

CHAPTER 2

Profitability, Accumulation and Industrial Capital

Abstract The very concept of capital refers to an articulation of three fundamental economic rhythms: the rhythm of valorisation, the rhythm of accumulation and the rhythm of realisation of value. Capitalist growth presupposes a relative compatibility between these three rhythms, while economic crises arise due to the excessive divergence of one of these rhythms in relation to the others. Every economic crisis can be described as an "organic arrhythmia" of the system. During the neoliberal period, the rate of profit (valorisation of value) recovers, but the rate of accumulation does not track the recovery in profitability: A divergence between the curve of the rate of profit and the curve of the rate of accumulation arises. The ratio Surplus Value (or Profit)/Accumulation grows.

Keywords Valorisation • Accumulation • Realisation • Rate of profit • Rate of accumulation • Surplus Value/Accumulation ratio

As shown in Charts 2.1, 2.2, 2.3, 2.4 and 2.5, during the neoliberal period, that is from the beginning of the 1980s onwards, labour productivity has been growing faster than real wages at the three major poles of the developed world: the USA, the EU-15 and Japan. This gap in productivity and real wage growth rates, in other words the increase of the exploitation rate of the labour force, is one of the fundamental characteristics of the neoliberal period. Contrary to that, productivity and

© The Author(s) 2019   13
S. Tombazos, *Global Crisis and Reproduction of Capital*, Palgrave
Insights into Apocalypse Economics,
https://doi.org/10.1007/978-3-030-05725-1_2

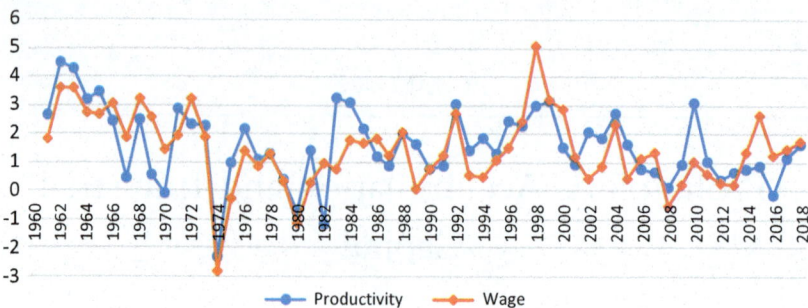

Chart 2.1   USA: Productivity and real wage growth (%), 1961–2018. Source: AMECO[1]

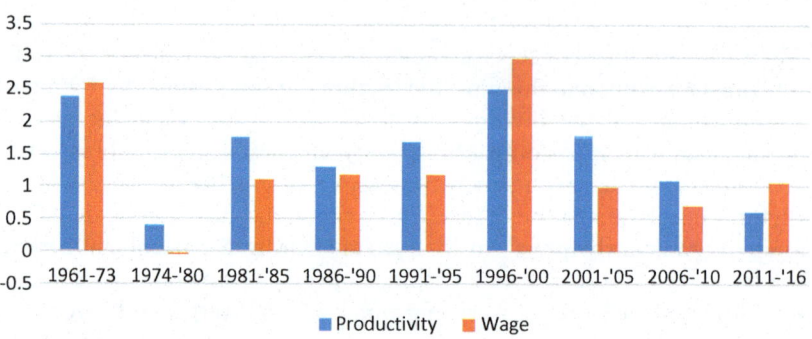

Chart 2.2   USA: Productivity and real wage growth (%), 1961–2016 Source: AMECO

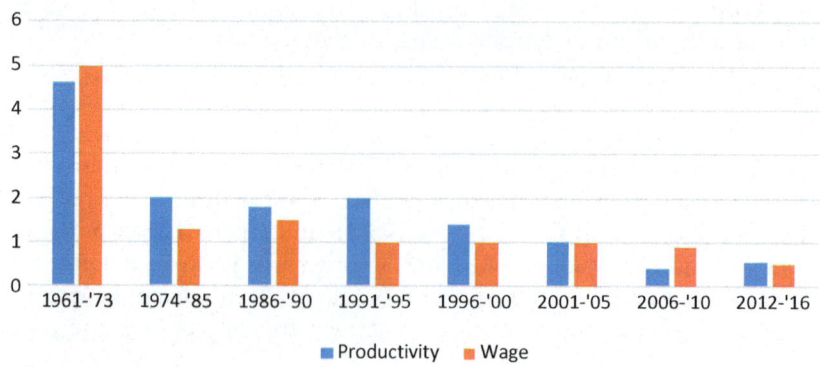

Chart 2.3   EU-15*: Productivity and real wage growth (%), 1961–2016.[2] Source: *European Economy, Statistical Annex*, Spring 2017. *Including West Germany for the period 1960–1990

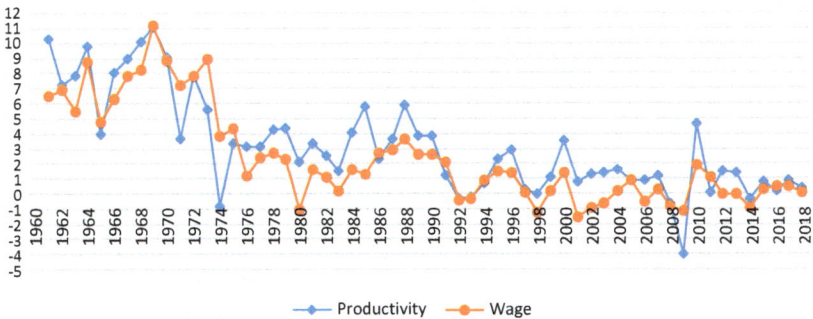

Chart 2.4 Japan: Productivity and real wage growth (%), 1961–2018. Source: AMECO

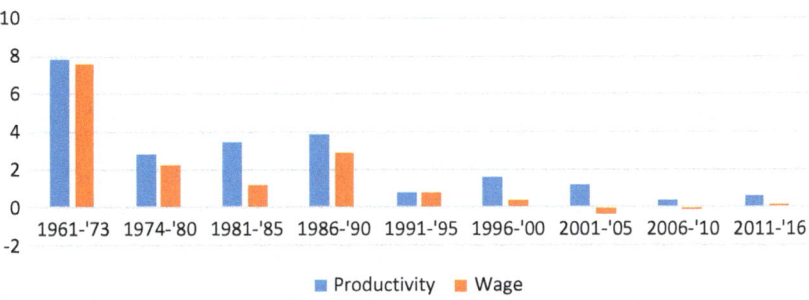

Chart 2.5 Japan: Productivity and real wage growth (%), 1961–2016. Source: AMECO

wages are rising almost in parallel in the first post-war period of Keynesian management, as shown clearly by the same charts for the period 1961–1973.

Capital attempted to respond to the fall in the rate of profit, which caused what some Marxist economists called the "long wave of depression" (Mandel, 1995), through policies aimed at increasing the rate of exploitation of labour power at all the three poles of the developed world. The rate of exploitation of labour power, that is the rate surplus value/variable capital (Sur/V), is one of the two components of the rate of profit. The other component is what Marx calls "organic composition of capital" (C/V), that is, the constant capital (C) on the variable capital (V). The rate of profit is the industrial profit or the surplus value on the total advanced capital amount:

$$\text{Rate of Profit} = \frac{\text{Sur}}{C+V} = \frac{\dfrac{\text{Sur}}{V}}{\dfrac{C}{V}+1}$$

In national and EU statistics, the profit rate (R) is the profit (PROF) on fixed capital (K): R = PROF/K (the fixed capital is Marx's constant capital after deducting from its value the part which is totally transferred to the commodity in each production cycle; for example, the value of the raw materials). This is not a problem for us; it simply means that the rate of profit (or "profitability") is calculated only for the most important component of Marx's denominator. The formula R = PROF/K can also be written in the following way: R = (PROF/GDP) × (GDP/K). The ratio PROF/GDP can be seen as an approximation of surplus value on variable capital (Sur/V). If PROF/GDP is increasing, the rate of exploitation of labour power (Sur/V) is increasing too. The ratio GDP/K, known as "capital productivity", can be seen as a reverse approximation of the organic composition of capital (V/C). The decrease in "capital productivity" is equivalent to an increase in the organic composition of capital (C/V).

The European Commission data on profitability (net return on net capital stock, total economy), which is presented in Charts 2.6, 2.7, 2.8 and 2.9, contains an important inaccuracy. Fixed capital was arbitrarily defined for the year 1960 (three times the GDP of each country or area), the year in which the calculation of profitability began. From that point, the fixed capital of year t equals the fixed capital of the previous year ($t-1$), adding to it the new investments in fixed capital and deducting depreciation (i.e. consumed fixed capital).

Taking into account this inaccuracy in the estimation of fixed capital for the year 1960, which influences the calculation of fixed capital for many years, Michel Husson (Husson, 2010) presented the evolution of profitability in four major economies—France, Germany (Schäfer, 2008; Weiß, 2015), USA (Duménil & Lévy, 2016) and UK—based on their national statistics. He shows that, although the rates of profit differ from those based on European Commission data, the evolution in each country is quite similar and does not affect the overall conclusions that one can draw from the figures. For this reason, we prefer to present here the European Commission data covering a large number of countries.

Let us also note that, year after year, the initial error in the estimation of the value of fixed capital in 1960 is progressively eliminated, and hence the deviation of national and the European Commission statistical data is decreasing. This is due to the calculation method of the value of fixed capital stock mentioned above: By subtracting depreciation and adding new fixed capital investments, year after year the initial error progressively decreases until it is completely eliminated. The time it takes for the initial error to be erased is equal to the rotation time of fixed capital.

As shown in Charts 2.6, 2.7, 2.8 and 2.9, capital profitability declined from the late 1960s in the USA and the EU-15. With some time lag, but with greater intensity, the same phenomenon can also be observed in

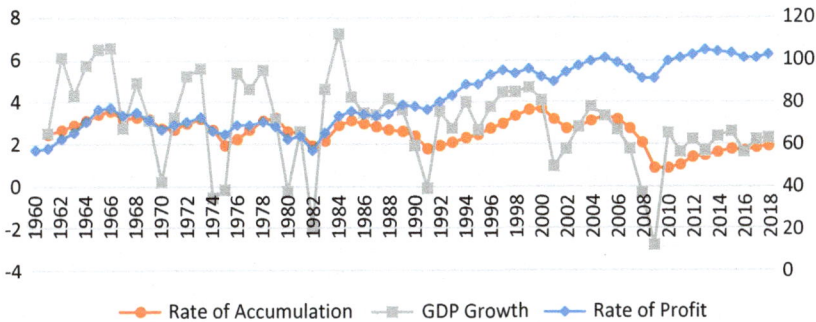

Chart 2.6   USA: Rate of profit (2010 = 100, right-hand scale, 1960–2018), rate of accumulation and GDP growth (%, 1961–2018). Source: AMECO

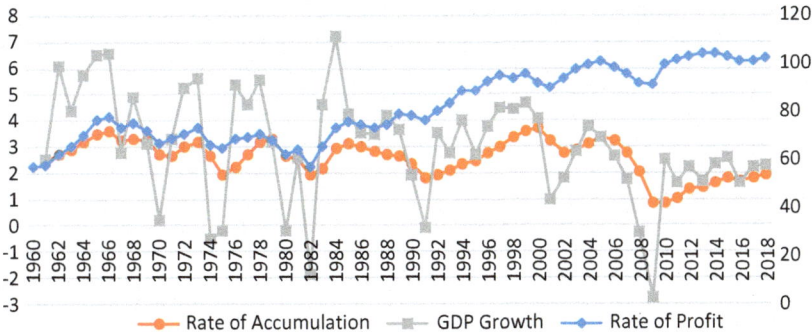

Chart 2.7   EU-15*: Rate of profit (2010 = 100, right-hand scale, 1960–2018), rate of accumulation and GDP growth (%, 1961–2018). Source: AMECO. *Including only West Germany for the period 1960–1990, except in the case of the calculation of the rate of profit

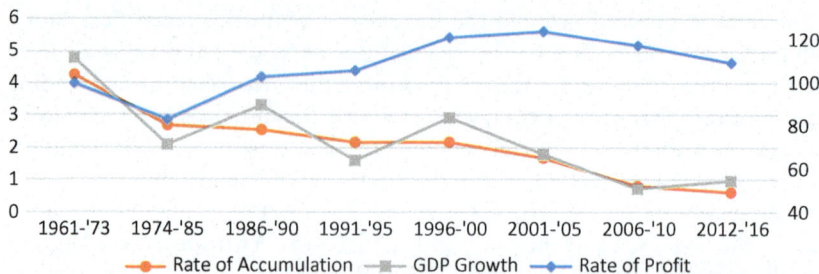

Chart 2.8 EU-15[*]: Rate of profit[3] (1961–1973 = 100, right-hand scale), rate of accumulation and GDP growth (%, 1961–2016). Source: *European Economy, Statistical Annex*, Spring 2017. [*]Including West Germany for the period 1960–1990

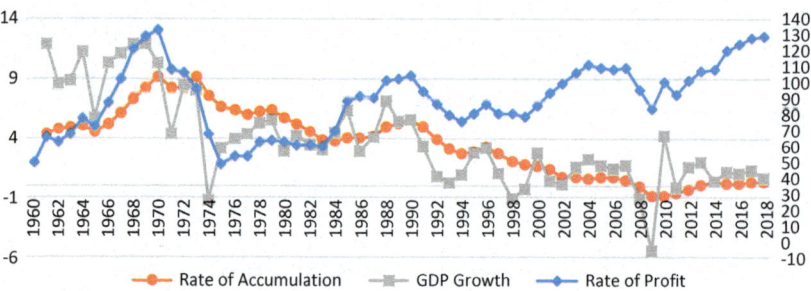

Chart 2.9 Japan: Rate of profit (2010 = 100, right-hand scale, 1960–2018), rate of accumulation and GDP growth (%, 1961–2018). Source: AMECO

Japan. From the early 1980s, however, despite fluctuations, profitability has recovered at the three major poles of the developed world.

Let us focus on the rate of profit during the years preceding the crisis. Profitability in the USA and the EU-15 had been slightly declining since 2005, but it was higher in 2008 than in 2001. In Japan, the fall in profitability starts a year earlier, but it remains higher in 2008 than in the early 2000s. In none of these cases is the fall in profitability able to explain the great recession of 2009. The fall in the rate of profit continues during the 2009 recession, but since 2010, the rate of profit starts to recover in all three major poles. While the economic crisis is perpetuated with all its known social consequences (unemployment, poverty, precariousness …), the rate of profit is rising: In 2013, in the USA and the EU-15, it appears to be at its highest point since 1960!

The Charts 2.6, 2.7, 2.8 and 2.9 also show the increase in fixed capital (which we call accumulation in Marxist terms) and GDP growth. In the case of the USA and the EU-15, the accumulation of capital closely follows the rate of profit from 1960 to the mid-1980s. Since then, however, a paradoxical divergence has appeared between the two variables: The accumulation of capital lags behind the recovery of the profit rate. The same divergence has appeared in Japan since the mid-1980s. As is logical and expected, at all three major poles of the developed economy, GDP growth follows the accumulation of capital.

The divergence of the profit and accumulation rates is crucial to understanding the neoliberal period in general and the current crisis in particular. This divergence cannot be disputed on the basis of the inaccurate estimation of the value of fixed capital in 1960, not only because the initial "error" is progressively decreasing, but also because it is confirmed by Charts 2.10, 2.11 and 2.12. The official data used in these charts have never been contested.

These three charts show the Surplus Value/Accumulation ratio. As the closest statistical concept to surplus value, we used the net operating surplus (net operating surplus, total economy). The net (of the value of the consumed fixed capital) operating surplus is the total profit (or surplus value), after deducting import and production taxes and adding subsidies, but before the total profit is divided in company profit, interest and dividend, that is before it takes the various forms that "industrial profit" may take according to Marx's terminology. For "accumulation", we used the

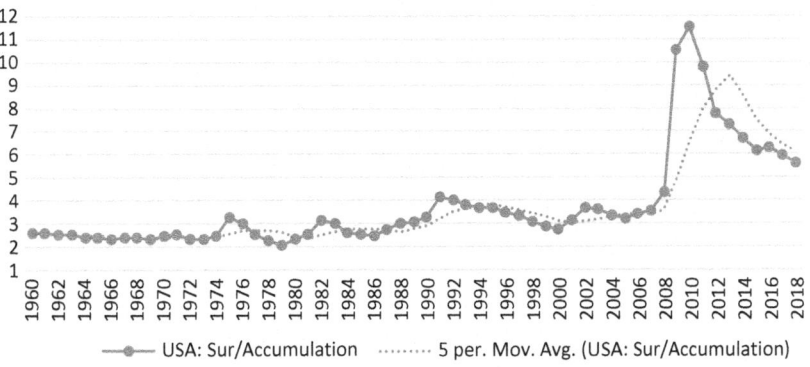

Chart 2.10 USA: Surplus Value/Accumulation Ratio, 1961–2018. Source: AMECO

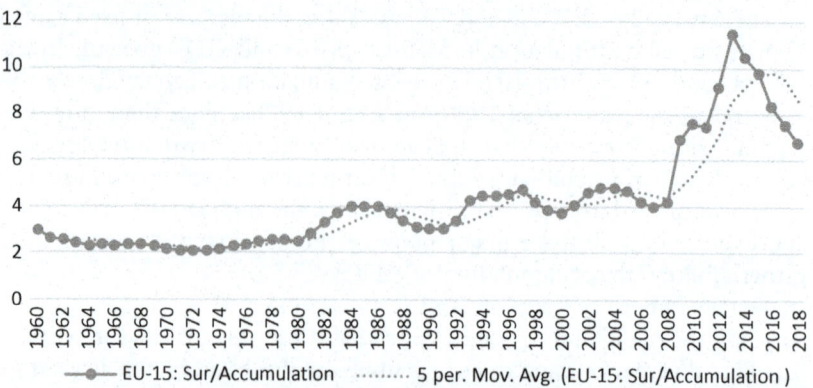

Chart 2.11   EU-15*: Surplus Value/Accumulation Ratio, 1960–2018. Source: AMECO. *Including West Germany for the period 1960–1990

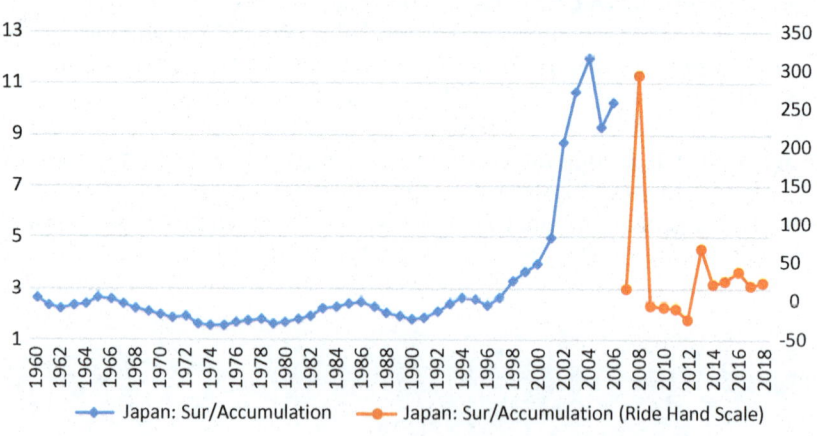

Chart 2.12   Japan: Surplus Value/Accumulation Ratio, 1960–2018. Source: AMECO

net (of the fixed capital depreciation) value of fixed capital added to the old one.

In the case of the USA, we have seen that the rate of profit diverges from the accumulation rate since the mid-1980s (Chart 2.10). Chart 2.10 confirms this discrepancy since the Surplus Value/Accumulation ratio from 2.51 in 1985 rises to 4.12 in 1991. In the 1990s, it gradually declined until 2000 (2.74 in this year). However, as we shall see later, the second half of the 1990s is a very special conjuncture for the USA: a very unusual conjuncture for the neoliberal period. After 2000, the Surplus Value/ Accumulation ratio rose steadily to reach 3.52 in 2007. In the 2009 recession and in the following year, the Surplus Value/Accumulation ratio reached historic levels: 10, 55 and 11.51, respectively.

In times of recession, it is normal for this ratio to increase as investment collapses. However, if one compares its growth during the years of the recession in the mid-1970s and the following few years and its rise after the great recession of 2009, one sees the difference between the Keynesian and the neoliberal period as concerns the trend of the capitalist class to invest in fixed capital.

In the case of the EU-15, Chart 2.11 clearly shows that the ratio of Surplus Value/Accumulation fluctuates in the 1980s at higher levels than in the two previous decades. Since then, it has been fluctuating at even higher levels. In the 1970s, it ranged between 2.04 and 2.55, between 2.84 and 4.00 in the 1980s, between 3.05 and 4.71 in the 1990s, between 4.00 and 7.59 in the 2000s. It peaked at 11.45 in 2013.

In Japan (Chart 2.12), the Surplus Value/Accumulation ratio increases in the period 1980–1995 compared to the previous period, especially in comparison to the 1970s. Since the mid-1990s, the upward trend of this ratio is so abrupt that it obliges us to change the scale in Chart 2.12 from 2007. In 2008, it reached 293.48 because fixed capital investment was extremely low. In 2009–2012, the ratio is negative because of fixed capital disinvestment. In other words, not only the surplus value is not invested at all in fixed capital, but the consumed fixed capital is not entirely replaced. Japan returns to positive rates of accumulation in 2013 but the Surplus Value/Accumulation ratio remains at very high levels in the following years (between 21.61 and 38.95).

At this point, it is possible to summarise some of the basic features of the neoliberal period:

1. The rate of surplus value (Sur/V) increases because labour productivity growth is higher than that of real wages.
2. According to official European data, the rate of profit, despite fluctuations, recovers from the 1970s when its decline was universal, albeit to varying degrees depending on the region. The evolution of the organic composition of capital (C/V) does not offset the increase of the surplus value rate (Sur/V).
3. However, the degree of "sensitivity" of fixed capital investment compared to the rate of profit clearly diminishes: The accumulation of capital does not closely follow the rate of profit. In other words,

capital requires greater profitability for the same rate of accumulation, as is clearly shown by the increase in the Surplus Value/ Accumulation ratio. Today's profits do not generate tomorrow's investment and economic growth: The assertion made to the contrary by former German Chancellor Helmut Smith has not been confirmed, and the "social democratic sacrifices" simply undermined trade union power, the labour acquis and, ultimately, social democracy itself, as the cases of France, Germany and Greece show.

4. And, of course, because surplus value is decreasingly invested in fixed capital, mass unemployment, precarious employment and poverty (that introduced what P. Bourdieu used to call "flexible exploitation") became fundamental social characteristics of neoliberal times.

Official data do not confirm a decrease in the rate of profit, but even if one contests these data, one cannot ignore the increasing gap between surplus value and accumulation. If one takes into consideration this gap, it is possible to understand the current crisis without using disputable data, that is without assuming any downward trend in the rate of profit during the neoliberal period.

Marx's theory of crises is undoubtedly not limited to the pages of the third volume (Marx, 1991) concerning the law of the downward trend of the rate of profit. As mentioned above, there is no systematic presentation of the crisis theory by Marx. Many elements that allow for a general understanding of capitalist crises are scattered throughout the three volumes of *Capital* and other books, especially the *Grundrisse* (Marx, 1973). However, some chapters in *Capital* are of particular interest for the theory of crises in general, and for the current crisis in particular.

The first four chapters of the second volume, which have not received the necessary attention, are of utmost importance because they demonstrate that Marx does not adopt a mono-causal interpretation of capitalist crises (Tombazos, 2014).

In these chapters, Marx presents and analyses what he calls "industrial capital" as the coexistence and simultaneous development of three vital capitalist processes, circles or circuits. These are the circuits of money capital, productive capital and commodity capital:

1. Circuit of Money Capital: M-C...P...C'-M'

Money (M) is transformed into productive capital (P) through the purchase of commodities (material means of production and labour power).

The production process, which is also the consumption of productive capital, produces new commodities of higher value (C') than those purchased (C), as they include surplus value. When sold, they are converted into money (M') of equal value. Therefore, M'–M = surplus value. In order to simplify his presentation, Marx initially considers that each stage of the circuit (M-C, P and C'-M') is completed before the next one starts, whereas in reality the three stages run simultaneously.

Marx believes that this circuit shows the capacity of capital to multiply itself through the production process and the exploitation of the labour power that takes place in it. Because the quantitative difference between the original M and the final M' is equal to the total surplus value produced or the total "industrial profit", this circuit pertains to the rhythm of valorisation of value.

2. Circuit of Productive Capital: $P...C'-M'-C^{(')}...P^{(')}$

Productive capital is transformed into commodities of greater value than the value of the means of production (including labour power) because they include surplus value. A share of this surplus value, however, necessarily escapes from the circuit because it is consumed privately by the capitalist. In the case of a simple reproduction of capital, the money (M) that will buy the necessary commodities (C) for the new production (the final P) does not contain any surplus value, since the industrialist entirely consumes it privately. Only in the case of expanded reproduction, apostrophes on the signs for the purchased commodity ($C^{(')}$) and for the new productive capital ($P^{(')}$) are needed. These apostrophes are put in brackets for two reasons: First, because they only apply in case of expanded reproduction; secondly, because the surplus value to which they refer is only a share of the total surplus value produced ($C'>C^{(')}$). In other terms, $P^{(')}-P=$ surplus value–share of surplus value privately consumed by the capitalist. Therefore, this circuit does not pertain to the rhythm of valorisation of value, but to the rhythm of accumulation of value, that is, to the rate of growth of productive capital.

3. Circuit of Commodity Capital: $C'-M'-C^{(')}...P^{(')}...C^{(')'}$

In this circuit, the process begins with the social recognition of the value contained in the commodity (C'). For this reason, Marx argues that this circuit pertains to the rhythm of realisation of value. In case of a simple reproduction of capital, the apostrophes in brackets are not needed for the same reasons mentioned above. In the case of expanded reproduction, the apostrophe in brackets in the final commodity ($C^{(\prime)\prime}$) indicates that its value, which contains the new surplus value produced, is greater than the value of the original commodity (C').

Industrial capital thus appears to Marx as an organisation of three fundamental economic rhythms: the rhythms of valorisation, accumulation and realisation of value. These rhythms are of course interdependent. Regular economic growth presupposes that they behave in a way that results in a relative "harmony" between them (as in music). If the rhythm of valorisation is too quick (i.e. the profit rate is too high) in comparison to the rhythm of realisation of value, such as in the 1929 crisis (i.e. the surplus value produced is not converted into money at the expected speed), the rhythm of valorisation is slowed down, decelerating also the rhythm of accumulation. In this case, the fall in the rate of profit is the result and not the cause of the crisis (Duménil & Lévy, 2011).[4]

If, therefore, capitalist growth is a convergence of rhythms, the economic crisis is nothing else than the manifestation of an economic discordance of rhythms or an economic "arrhythmia". The latter results from a conjunctural "autonomization" (*Verselbständigung*) of one fundamental economic rhythm in relation to the other two.

Very explicitly, Marx analyses capitalist crises as an economic "arrhythmia" in the first four chapters of the second volume of *Capital*. In order to follow him in detail, it is useful to "simplify" the three circuits of industrial capital. Marx himself presents the three circuits with symbols (M, C, etc.) so that each one includes five terms. This presentation has the advantage of being very descriptive and hence easily understood, but it creates some problems that force Marx to abandon it, in words and not in symbols, when analysing capitalist crises.

The biggest problem with this presentation is the following: Each circuit contains five terms. However, they do not have equal status. Only three of them are functional in each circuit. Therefore, we need to turn the descriptive circuits of capital into its functional circuits by deleting the "passive" terms.

Marx's formula for the circuit of money capital is M-C...P...C'-M'. However, the first C does not function as commodity in this circuit, because it will not be sold in its present form. C simply indicates the function of the original M, which buys the means of production from another capital and from the working class. This commodity (C) is "passive" in our circuit and can be deleted. M' can also be deleted because it simply indicates the function of C' that consists in its conversion into money. Of course, a part of M' (not the entire M') will function again as capital, not in this specific circuit but in the following circuit of money capital. For the same reasons, one can eliminate the last term in the other two circuits of capital, as well as the commodity that does not function as such in each of them.

We can now present the three functional circuits of industrial capital (to avoid complications with the apostrophes, let us first assume that we have a simple reproduction of capital):

Simple reproduction of capital	
Descriptive circuits	Functional circuits
M-C...P...C'-M'	M...P...C'
P...C'-M'-C...P	P...C'-M
C'-M'-C...P... C'	C'-M...P

One detail has to be clarified here. Because in the new transcription of the three circuits we are interested in the functional forms of capital, we transcribe the M' of productive capital's and commodity capital's descriptive circuits as M (without apostrophe). In these two descriptive circuits, M' represents the transformation of C', but the entire surplus value contained in money, in simple reproduction of capital, will escape from the circuits to be spent privately by the capitalist.

In expanded reproduction of capital, the only modification needed is to place the apostrophes in brackets in the circuits of productive capital and commodity capital:

Expanded reproduction of capital	
Descriptive circuits	Functional circuits
M-C...P...C'-M'	M...P...C'
P...C'-M'-C$^{(')}$...P$^{(')}$	P...C'-M$^{(')}$
C'-M'-C$^{(')}$...P$^{(')}$... C$^{(')'}$	C'- M$^{(')}$...P$^{(')}$

Capitalist reproduction thus appears as a continuous sequence of the three functional forms of capital that coexist at each moment as a result of the cycle of its transformations. More analytically, as Marx writes:

The total circuit presents itself for each functional form of capital as its own specific circuit, and indeed each of these circuits conditions the continuity of the overall process; the circular course of one functional form determines that of the others. It is a necessary condition for the overall production process, in other words [*besonders* in the original language: this means "especially" and not "in other words"][5] for the social capital, that this is at the same time a process of reproduction, and hence the circuit of each of its moments. Different fractions of the capital successively pass through the different stages and functional forms. Each functional form thus passes through its circuit simultaneously with the others, though it is always a different part of the capital that presents itself in it. A part of the capital exists as commodity capital that is being transformed into money, but this is an ever-changing part, and is constantly being reproduced; another part exists as money capital that is being transformed into productive capital; a third part as productive capital being transformed into commodity capital. The constant presence of all three forms is mediated by the circuit of the total capital through precisely these three phases. (Marx, 1992, p. 184)

Hence, industrial capital, this "abstraction in action" as Marx writes[6] (Marx, 1992, p. 185), is a continuous process in which its functional forms manifest themselves as "fluid forms, and their simultaneity is mediated by their succession" (Marx, 1992, p. 184). In other words, we must read the three circuits of each individual capital, and certainly of social capital, not only horizontally (as a transformation or metamorphosis of each functional form) but also vertically (as the simultaneous coexistence of each functional form). The succession of the functional forms results in their simultaneous coexistence. In times of crisis, the incompatibility of the three rhythms of capital, their "arrhythmia", manifests itself as a disproportion between the three functional forms of capital that coexist simultaneously.

The divergence between the rate of profit and the rate of accumulation of capital results in excessive liquidity at the disposal of the capitalist class, which invests in fixed capital an ever decreasing share of the total surplus value.

Nevertheless, this excessive liquidity does not yet explain anything. One could say, for example, that part of the surplus value escapes to third countries, especially to developing countries, to be invested there. Doubtlessly, this happens mainly in the form of foreign direct investment, but the developing countries also finance the developed world by investing their foreign exchange reserves (China), servicing their public and private foreign debt and so forth. Without having to provide data on global capital flows, we know that the industrial profit (i.e. total surplus value) is decreasingly invested in fixed capital, leading to another interesting divergence: Private consumption as a share of GDP seems to change independently of the wage share in GDP. Hence, since the 1980s, the ratio Private Consumption/Wage Share is increasing in all the major regions of the developed world.

NOTES

1. Data from AMECO were retrieved in November 2017. Data for 2017 and 2018 are estimates/forecasts from the European Commission (this applies to all charts based on this source).
2. The periodisation for the EU-15 is somewhat different from Charts 2.2 and 2.5 because, on the basis of the available data on the AMECO website, it is not possible to calculate the two variables (productivity and wage) for the whole period, due to the fact that some data include only West Germany before the unification of West Germany and East Germany. For this reason, we use the data as they appear at *European Economy, Statistical Annex*, Spring 2017: https://ec.europa.eu/info/files/statistical-annex-european-economy-spring-2017_en
3. Because in Chart 2.7, the calculation of the rate of profit took into account Germany (not only West Germany), and although this inaccuracy has little effect on the profitability curve, we show the evolution of the same variables presented in this chart also in Chart 2.8, based on *European Economy, Statistical Data*, Spring 2017.
4. They argue that the 1929 crisis and the present crisis, unlike the crisis of the1970s, cannot be attributed to the fall in the rate of profit.
5. The "circular course of one functional form determines that of the others. It is a necessary condition for the overall production process", not only for the social capital but also for the individual capital.
6. "Capital, as self-valorizing value, does not just comprise class relations, a definite social character that depends on the existence of labour as wage-labour. It is a movement, a circulatory process through different stages, which itself in turn includes three different forms of the circulatory process. Hence it can only be grasped as a movement, and not as a static thing. Those who consider the autonomization [*Verselbstständigung*] of value as a mere abstraction forget that the movement of industrial capital is this abstraction in action. Here value passes through different forms, different movements in which it is both preserved and increases, is valorized".

BIBLIOGRAPHY

Duménil, G., & Lévy, D. (2011). *The Crisis of Neoliberalism*. Cambridge, MA: Harvard University Press.

Duménil, G., & Lévy, D. (2016). *The Historical Trends of Technology and Distribution in the U.S. Economy: Data and figures (since 1869)*. Retrieved from: http://www.cepremap.fr/membres/dlevy/biblioa.htm

Husson, M., (2010, January). La hausse tendancielle du taux de profit. Retrieved from: http://hussonet.free.fr/tprof9.pdf

Mandel, E. (1995). *Long Waves of Capitalist Development: A Marxist Interpretation*. London, New York: Verso.

Marx, K. (1973). *Grundrisse: Foundations of the Critique of Political Economy (Rough Draft)*. London, New York: Penguin Books.

Marx, K. (1991). *Capital: A Critique of Political Economy*. Volume Three. London, New York: Penguin Books.

Marx, K. (1992). *Capital: A Critique of Political Economy*. Volume Two. London, New York: Penguin Books.

Schäfer, C. (2008). *Anhaltende Verteilungsdramatik. WSI-Verteilungsbericht 2008*. Retrieved from: http://www.boeckler.de/pdf/wsimit_2008_11_schaefer.pdf

Tombazos, S. (2014). *Time in Marx. The Categories of Time in Marx's Capital*. Leiden, Boston: Brill Academic Publisher.

Weiß, T. (2015, October 22–24). The rate of return on capital in Germany—an empirical study. 19th FMM Conference: *The Spectre of Stagnation? Europe in the World Economy*, Berlin Steglitz: Retrieved from: https://www.boeckler.de/pdf/v_2015_10_24_weiss.pdf

CHAPTER 3

Private Consumption, Wage Share of GDP and Reproduction Schemas

Abstract The financial system of the neoliberal period has allowed the massive "transfer" of future demand by wage earners to the present time through rising debt, whose servicing has increasingly undermined the disposable part of their wages for consumption. Marx's schemas of extended reproduction are modified to show that borrowing stimulates consumption, which has a positive effect on investment and employment, thus leading to greater production. However, these reproduction schemas are structurally unstable and from the outset have an expiration date. They collapse, once the so-called markets begin to doubt whether the accumulated rights on future wages will be redeemed. Thus, the economic crisis manifests itself initially in its financial dimension, as an accumulation of unsustainable private debts.

Keywords Reproduction schemas • Future demand • Private debt • Debt service • Disposable income

During the neoliberal period, as clearly shown in Charts 3.1, 3.2 and 3.3, private consumption (as a share of GDP) does not evolve alongside the adjusted wage share of GDP. The wage share is statistically "adjusted" to offset the impact of the income of the self-employed, to whom the average wage is attributed. Hence, the adjusted wage share of GDP is an indicator that allows comparison between different times and different countries:

© The Author(s) 2019   29
S. Tombazos, *Global Crisis and Reproduction of Capital*, Palgrave
Insights into Apocalypse Economics,
https://doi.org/10.1007/978-3-030-05725-1_3

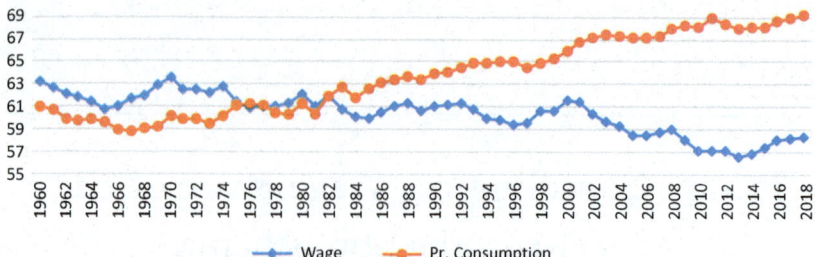

Chart 3.1   USA: Adjusted wage share and private consumption (% of GDP), 1960–2018. Source: AMECO

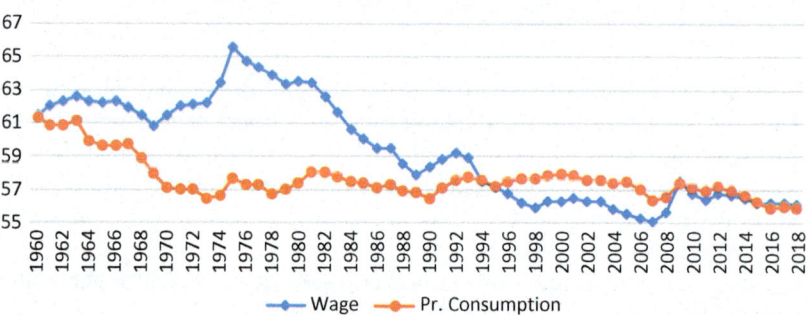

Chart 3.2   EU-15*: Adjusted wage share and private consumption (% of GDP), 1960–2018. Source: AMECO. *Including West Germany for the period 1960–1990

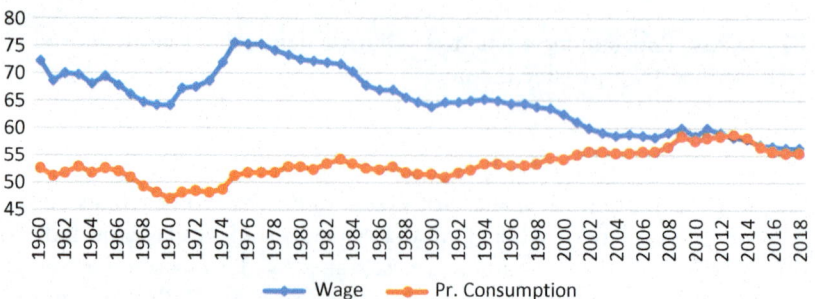

Chart 3.3   Japan: Adjusted wage share and private consumption (% of GDP), 1960–2018. Source: AMECO

An increase in the adjusted wage share of GDP in a country indicates faster wage growth than GDP growth, that is, a more favourable income distribution for the working class or a decrease in the exploitation rate of the labour power.

Since the early 1980s, at all three major poles of the world economy, the ratio Private Consumption/Wage Share of GDP is increasing (Chart 3.4). Of course, at least at first sight, this increase is due to different reasons. In the USA, private consumption (Chart 3.1) is increasing, while the wage share of GDP declines slightly until the early 2000s. In the EU-15, on the other hand, private consumption is relatively stable, while the wage share of GDP decreases considerably since the mid-1970s (Chart 3.2).

To a certain extent, this difference between the two cases is due to the fact that in the USA there is a high proportion of high incomes in the total income recorded as salaries. According to some authors (Dew-Becker & Cordon, 2005), the "superstar economy" alters the evolution of the wage share of GDP: Some of the distributed profits deriving from certain economic activities, such as the income of the golden boys of the financial system and other superstars of cinema and sport, which in fact constitutes a kind of rent, are treated by the statistical authorities as "salary". As a result, if the top 5% of "wages" is not taken into account when calculating the wage share of GDP, its curve in the US case would be similar to that of the EU-15 case.

In any case, what really matters is that the ratio Private Consumption/Wage Share of GDP increases everywhere from the early 1980s: As shown in Chart 3.4, the three curves of this ratio evolve quite similarly, although

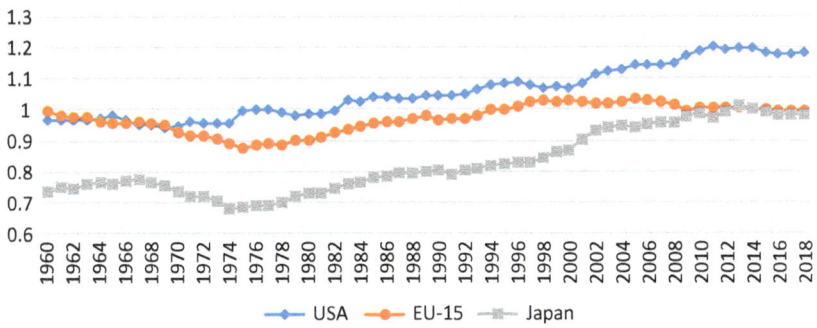

Chart 3.4   USA, EU-15, Japan: Private Consumption/Wage Ratio, 1960–2018. Source: AMECO

the curve concerning Japan (see also Chart 3.3 for Japan) starts from a lower level.

What exactly does the increase in the ratio Private Consumption/Wage Share of GDP depend on? It depends on four key factors:

1. On the increase in the net capital inflow in the country, which affects the available liquidity in the economy. When a country has a deficit in current transactions, this deficit can only be financed from abroad.
2. On the reduction in the savings rate of households.
3. On the increase in the share of industrial profit that the owners of the means of production consume privately.
4. On the increase in the share of industrial profit transferred to the middle- or lower-income strata (self-employed, workers, etc.) in the form of consumer credit.

As regards the first factor, Chart 3.5 shows that during the neoliberal period, there is a net inflow of capital (current account in deficit) in the USA, but not in Japan, which has a net outflow of capital (current account in surplus). The EU-15 presents a more "balanced" capital inflow-outflow (before the crisis) because its current account balance is generally around zero. Hence, if the available liquidity in the US economy is increasing because of capital inflows from Japan, the available liquidity for private consumption is decreasing in Japan. Nevertheless, the ratio Private Consumption/Wage Share of GDP increases in both cases.

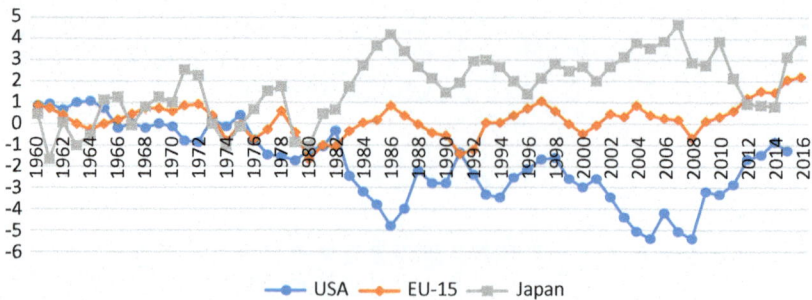

Chart 3.5 USA*, EU-15** and Japan: current account (% of GDP), 1960–2016. Source: AMECO. *1960–2015, **Including West Germany for the period 1960–1990

As regards the second factor, the household savings rate is clearly declining in the USA and Japan, especially in the last years before the crisis, but this is not the case in the Eurozone, where its decrease is very small (Charts 3.6, 3.7 and 3.8).

The third factor does not automatically or necessarily lead to financial instability. One could imagine a relatively stable schema of slowed economic growth where a larger share of industrial profit is consumed in luxury products whose "specific weight" in the whole production is adjusted accordingly.

Economic instability arises when profits that are not productively invested are les and les consumed by the classes that appropriate them. Consequently, the fourth factor that explains the increasing trend of the ratio Private Consumption/Wage Share of GDP merits all our attention.

If wages freeze while the debt of working-class households is constantly on the rise, wage earners spend some of their future income at the present time. This debt may be sustainable as long as the working-class people's ability to service it is not justifiably or unjustifiably challenged by the "markets". In the event of such a challenge, the whole model of development (or the schema of reproduction) collapses because the subjectivities that formed it (the "markets") realise the fragile nature of its foundations. The ensuing panic leads to a financial crisis with the first obvious cracks in the model's foundations.

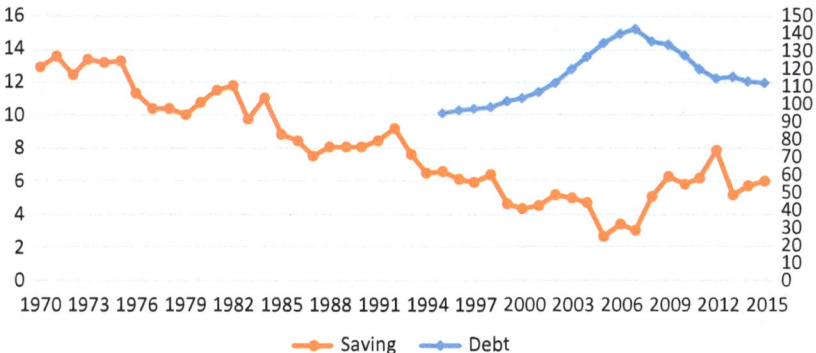

Chart 3.6   USA: Household debt (1995–2015, right-hand scale) and household savings (1970–2015) as percentage of net disposal income. Source: OECD (https://data.oecd.org/hha/household-savings.htm   and   https://data.oecd. org/hha/household-debt.htm)

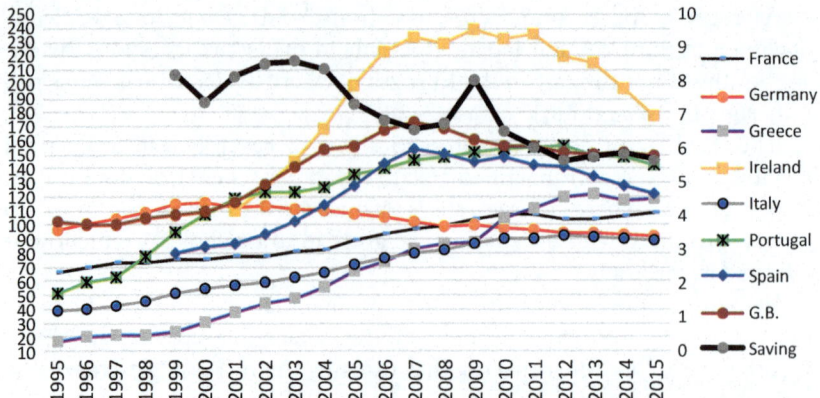

Chart 3.7 Household debt (1995–2015*) in some European countries and household savings in Eurozone (1999–2015, right-hand scale) as percentage of net disposal income. Source: OECD (https://data.oecd.org/hha/household-savings.htm and https://data.oecd.org/hha/household-debt.htm). *Ireland: 2001–2015. Spain: 1999–2015

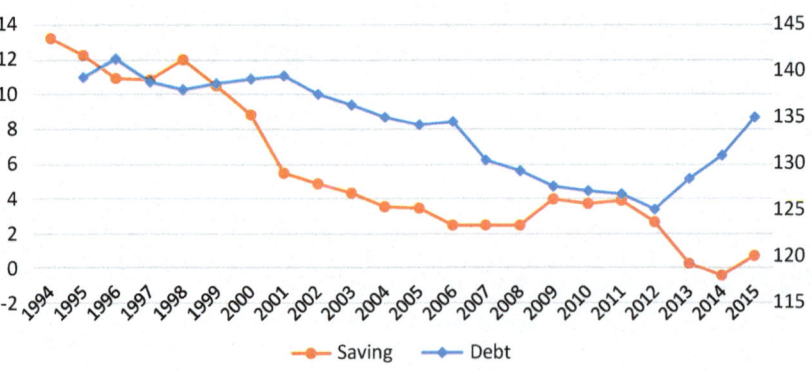

Chart 3.8 Japan: Household debt (1995–2015, right-hand scale) and household savings (1994–2015) as percentage of net disposal income. Source: OECD (https://data.oecd.org/hha/household-savings.htm and https://data.oecd.org/hha/household-debt.htm)

Charts 3.6, 3.7 and 3.8 show the net household savings[1] rate as a percentage of household real net disposable income[2] and the evolution of household debt as a percentage of household real net disposable income. In all the countries presented (and in all the economically important countries of Europe not shown: the Netherlands, Belgium, Sweden, Denmark, Finland, Austria), with the exception of Germany and Japan, household debt increased during the years preceding the crisis.

Of course, statistics do not separate households according to the social strata to which they belong. However, taking into account the data presented in Charts 2.10, 2.11 and 2.12, we know that households that appropriate the surplus value invest a decreasing share of it in fixed capital. Hence, they are awash with liquidity. Of course, some of the ruling-class households borrow to invest in the stock market, in real estate and so forth, but to the extent they do so, they borrow money from other ruling-class households through the banking system. The question is where the surplus value not invested in fixed capital is really going. The increase in household debt also results from the increase in working-class household debt. This is the reason why household debt is increasing alongside the ratio Private Consumption/Wage Share of GDP.

It is worth noting that the purchase of real estate is always recorded in statistics as "investment" and not as "consumption", despite the fact that, for example, the purchase of a house for one's own use should be considered as private "consumption". Buying real estate for one's own use is not economically different from buying a household appliance. Therefore, the increase in household debt does not necessary imply an increase in the ratio Private Consumption/Wage Share of GDP. If this ratio shows an upward trend, it is because the working-class households borrow not only to buy real estate but also to increase their "ordinary" consumption (the consumption recorded as such by statistics).

Of course, not all countries are included in this general scheme in the same way. In Japan and Germany, there is no increase in household debt in the years preceding the crisis. This demonstrates the export orientation of these countries: Because they seek and achieve surpluses in their foreign trade, they export part of their savings to other countries of the developed world. Given that a substantial share of Japanese surplus value is invested in the USA, a share of US surplus value is "liberated" and can be lent in the form of consumer credit (including mortgages). Looking closely at Chart 3.7, it will be noticed that household debt is growing faster from the late 1990s in the southern European countries—Spain, Portugal,

Greece and Ireland (which is also a south European economy from the economic point of view)—compared to the three largest economies in the Eurozone (Germany, France, Italy). This means that some of the surplus value produced in Germany and other northern Eurozone countries with current account surpluses is invested in the southern Eurozone (and other countries outside the Eurozone). This does not mean that a country like France with a relatively balanced current account in the 2000s before the crisis does not invest in a country like Greece. The surplus value that France invests in Greece can be, for example, the "liberated" French surplus value through the investment of German surplus value in France.

The fact that the capital inflows in the developed world are more important than the capital outflows does not apply to each developed country or region separately. It means, however, that it is not possible to interpret the gap between the rate of profit and the rate of accumulation of fixed capital or the increase in the ratio of Surplus Value/Accumulation through the outflow of surplus value from the developed world. A greater share of the developed world's surplus value results in private consumption through the increase in working-class borrowing.

Based on the reproduction schemas of capital developed by Marx, we will show that a reproduction schema based on increasing working-class indebtedness is not sustainable in the long run. We will show that in the neoliberal reproduction schema, as it has evolved from the early 1980s, the threat of collapse was present from the beginning. Its realisation was just a matter of time.

A capitalist model of development is what Marx calls "schema of reproduction of capital". The second volume of *Capital* (Marx, 1992) begins with a first section that, as we have seen, analyses the three basic rhythms of capital. In the process of reproduction of social capital, some quantitative relations between its three functional forms that coexist simultaneously must be respected. In the last section of the second volume, in very general terms, Marx attempts to determine these quantitative relations or necessary proportions between these functional forms (money capital, productive capital and commodity capital). Thus, a general idea of the schemas of reproduction of industrial capital is formulated. The circuit best suited to the development of such reproductive schemas is the third circuit of industrial capital, that is the circuit of commodity capital or the circuit of realisation of value: $C'-M'-C^{(')}...P^{(')}... C^{(')}$.

The basic idea is as follows: A schema of reproduction of capital can perpetuate itself only if the supply of commodity values of the various productive departments corresponds to a distribution of social incomes that more or less ensures the realisation of the commodity values under conditions of simple or expanded reproduction of capital. This means that distribution of money in the form of income, distribution of productive activities and hence distribution of particular commodities in a social formation are interdependent. Let us give a very simple example: If the value of commodities for working-class consumption cannot be socially realised or recognised because the social distribution of income does not allow their purchase at their value, the rhythm of realisation of value decelerates. The three rhythms of capital are not compatible with each other. The economic crisis is nothing else than this "arrhythmia".

The examples developed by Marx divide productive activity into two departments: Department I that produces commodities for productive consumption (the means of production except labour power), and Department II that produces commodities for private consumption.

The value of the annual product of Department I (Ia), which produces the material means of production, includes the consumed constant capital (Ic), the consumed variable capital (Iv) and the surplus value ($Isur$): $Ia = Ic + Iv + Isur$.

By analogy, the annual value of Department II, which produces consumer commodities, is written as follows: $IIa = IIc + IIv + IIsur$.

In conditions of simple reproduction, to the supply of means of production (Ia) corresponds the demand $Ic + IIc$, because capitalists should simply replace the productively consumed constant capital. So, $Ic + Iv + Isur = Ic + IIc$. By deleting the equivalent terms appearing on both sides of the equation, we see that the net added value of Department I should correspond to the demand for constant capital of Department II: $Iv + Isur = IIc$.

Starting from the supply of Department II, we will end up in exactly the same equation (with reversal of the left and right legs). Who buys these commodities? The capitalists of both departments with the surplus value they appropriate, as well as their workers with their wages. Consequently, $IIc + IIv + IIsur = Isur + IIsur + Iv + IIv$. Deleting the equivalent terms on both sides of the equation, we see that the supply of Department II corresponding to its constant capital must be equal to the demand from Department I corresponding to the wages ("labour cost of the product") and its surplus value: $IIc = Iv + Isur$.

Under conditions of expanded reproduction, part of the surplus value will be productively invested in constant capital in both departments (ic

and *iic*). Therefore, another part of the surplus value has to be invested in additional variable capital (*iv* and *iiv*), and only the surplus value remaining will be consumed privately by the capitalists (*ip* and *iip*). Therefore, the surplus value in each department is now divided into three parts as follows: $Isur = ic + iv + ip$ and $IIsur = iic + iiv + iip$. Therefore, the value of the supply (left-hand side of the equation) and the value of the demand (right-hand side) of Department I and Department II can now be written as follows:

Department I: $Ic + Iv + ic + iv + ip = Ic + ic + IIc + iic$ or $\boldsymbol{Iv + iv + ip = IIc + iic}$.

The part of the value offered by Department I to Department II, including its variable capital, the surplus value transformed in additional variable capital and the surplus value consumed privately by the capitalists, must correspond to the demand of Department II in constant capital.

Department II: $\boldsymbol{IIc + IIv + iic} \mid iiv + iip = Iv + iv + ip + IIv + iiv + iip$ or $\boldsymbol{IIc + iic = Iv + iv + ip}$.

The part of the value corresponding to the supply of Department II to Department I, including its constant capital and its additional constant capital (the new investment in constant capital), must be equal to the total demand of Department I for consumer commodities.

There is no doubt that these schemas of reproduction operate at a high level of abstraction. They constitute a very simplified understanding of reality. There is also no doubt that they do not aim to prove either that the system will collapse after a number of reproduction periods or that it will be forever reproduced. As argued elsewhere (Tombazos, 2014), Marxists who argued for the collapse, as well as those who saw the possibility of endless capitalist development in these reproduction schemas, fall under the same methodological error. Marx puts the whole issue in a different way: In order for capitalist reproduction to be relatively smooth, the reproduction schemas must respect the aforementioned equilibrium conditions.

The reproduction of capital that we have already implicitly suggested changes the schemas developed by Marx as follows: In conditions of expanded reproduction, part of the total surplus value of both departments is neither productively invested by the capitalists nor consumed privately by them, but is granted as a loan to the wage earners. Consequently, to the consumption corresponding to the wages of each period ($Iv + IIv + iv + iiv$), we must add the consumption corresponding to loans granted to the workers (glw) in the current or previous periods, and deduct the debt service (dsw) of the current period.

Workers' consumption during the current period can now be written as follows: $Iv + IIv + iv + iiv + glw - dsw$. Their total consumption increases so long as glw is greater than dsw.

The glw-surplus value stimulates the demand for consumer commodities. However, to the extent that the glw-surplus value is returned to capital through gradual debt service, the rate of capital accumulation must accelerate in both productive departments, that is the productive consumption of constant and variable capital must increase in both departments. The supply and demand equilibrium of consumer goods and means of production is now achieved at a higher level of production.

Let us call the glw-surplus value that is returned to the capitalist through the gradual debt service (for loans of the current and prior periods) $rglw$. This rglw-surplus value will be invested in the two departments. One part of this amount will be invested in additional constant and variable capital in Department I ($icrglw$ and $ivrglw$), and the other part in additional constant and variable capital in Department II ($iicrglw$ and $iivrglw$). The equilibrium equation of each department can now be rewritten as follows:

Department I :

$Ic + Iv + ic + iv + ip + icrglw + ivrglw = Ic + IIc + ic + iic + icrglw + iicrglw$ or
$Iv + iv + ip + ivrglw = IIc + iic + iicrglw$

The lending creates an additional supply ($ivrglw$) from Department I to Department II and a corresponding additional demand ($iicrglw$) of Department II for Department I: **$ivrglw = iicrglw$**.

Department II :

$IIc + IIv + iic + iiv + iip + iicrglw + iivrglw = Iv + IIv + iv + iiv + ip + iip$
$+ glw - dsw$ or $IIc + iic + iicrglw + iivrglw = Iv + iv + ip + glw - dsw$

Lending also creates an additional supply in consumer commodities ($iicrglw + iivrglw$) and a corresponding additional demand ($glw - dsw$):

$iicrglw + iivrglw = glw - dsw$. Given that $ivrglw = iicrglw$, we know that $glw - dsw = ivrglw + iivrglw$. Therefore:

$$IIc + iic + iicrglw + iivrglw = Iv + iv + ip + ivrglw + iivrglw \text{ or}$$

$$\textbf{\textit{IIc}} + \textbf{\textit{iic}} + \textbf{\textit{iicrglw}} = \textbf{\textit{Iv}} + \textbf{\textit{iv}} + \textbf{\textit{ip}} + \textbf{\textit{ivrglw}}$$

Just as in Marx's reproduction schemas, the supply from Department I to Department II corresponds to the demand of Department II for means of production, while the supply of Department II to Department I corresponds to the demand of Department I for consumer goods.

Lending acts as a multiplier of production, investment and wages and/ or employment. However, such a reproduction schema is only sustainable in the long run if debt service does not undermine wages: In this case, granting loans to workers becomes more and more risky for the capitalists.

If we assume, simplifying our presentation, that the exploitation rate (Sur/V) and the share of the surplus value allocated as a loan to total surplus value (glw/Sur) do not change, and if the time to pay back the loan with its interest (Int) is equal to one period (t), then we will have the following sequence:

Period	t_1	t_2	t_3	$...t_n$
Loan amount	glw_1	$glw_2 + Int_1$	$glw_3 + Int_1 + Int_2$	$glw_n + Int_1 + Int_2 ... + Int_{n-1}$
Debt service[a]	$glw_1 + Int_1$	$glw_2 + Int_1 + Int_2$	$glw_3 + Int_1 + Int_2 + Int_3$	$glw_n + Int_1 + Int_2 ... + Int_n$

[a]Corresponding to the loan amount, regardless of whether the debt service is not completed in the same period but in the next one

If we deduct the loan amount of each period from the debt service that corresponds to it, we will have the following sequence:

Period	t_1	t_2	t_3	$...t_n$
Interest	Int_1	Int_2	Int_3	$... Int_n$

However, the loan amount increases disproportionately to the glw-surplus value from period to period because it includes the accumulated interest of the previous periods. In other words, the increase in the interest from period to period not only corresponds to the increase in glw-surplus value, but also to the cumulative interest of the previous periods. With a fixed interest rate (e), we can write the interest corresponding to the loan amount of each period as follows:

Period	t_1	t_2	t_3	$...t_n$
Interest	$e.glw_1$	$(e.glw_2)+(e.Int_1)$	$(e.glw_3)+[e.$ $(Int_1+Int_2)]$	$(e.glw_n)+[e.$ $(Int_1+Int_2...+Int_{n-1})]$

Consequently, capital gains (interest) added to the surplus value increasingly undermine the purchasing power of wages. In order for a reproduction schema to include a transfer of a part of the surplus value to wage labour in the form of a loan, the debt service should not rise continuously disproportionately to wages. However, given that debt service rises (in relation to the total borrowed amount) more than the increase in glw-surplus value, the Debt Service/Wage ratio rises constantly. In other words, the share of the total wage available for consumption constantly decreases. Here is a numerical example:

Period	t_1	t_2	t_3	t_4
Sur/V	100/100	105/105	110,25/110,25	115,7625/115,7625
Loan amount	$glw_1 = 20$	$glw_2+Int_1 =$ $21+1=22$	$glw_3+Int_1+Int_2 =$ $22,05+1+1,1=24,15$	$glw_4+Int_1+Int_2+$ $Int_3 = 23,1525$ $+1+1,1$ $+1,2075= 26,46$
Debt service	$glw_1+Int_1 =$ $20+1=21$	glw_2+Int_1 $+Int_2 = 21$ $+1+1,1 = 23,1$	$glw_3+Int_1+Int_2$ $+Int_3 = 22,05+1$ $+1,1+1,2075 =$ $25,3575$	$glw_4+Int_1+Int_2+Int_3+$ $Int_4 = 23,1525+1+1,1$ $+1,2075+1323=27,783$
Debt service/V	21%	22%	23%	24%

Assumptions: Sur / V = 100%, glw / Sur = 20%, Period of Debt Service = t, e = 5%, Rate of growth of Sur and V (V = wage) from period to period = 5%

The reproduction schema we present, in some of its assumptions, is much more "conservative" than reality because, as we have shown, the exploitation rate of labour power $\left(\dfrac{\text{Sur}}{V}\right)$ is increasing during the neoliberal period. It is also unlikely that the growth rate of glw-surplus value will not register an upward trend, since from the outset it arises from the relative saturation of the private consumption of the capitalists and the increase in the ratio of Surplus Value/Accumulation.

Such an unbalanced reproduction schema will exhaust its absolute time horizon as soon as the proportion of disposable wages shrinks to such an extent that the reproduction of labour power is no longer compatible with debt service. This time horizon is "inversely proportional" to the following variables:

1. Increase in the rate of surplus value (Sur/V).
2. Increase in the ratio Glw-Surplus Value/Surplus Value.
3. Increase in the interest rate (e).
4. Reduction in the debt service period.

It collapses, however, before exhausting its absolute horizon: once the so-called markets start to doubt whether the accumulated rights on future wages will be redeemed. The economic crisis thus manifests itself first in its financial dimension as the accumulation of unsustainable private debts.

The financial system of the neoliberal period allowed the massive "transfer" of future working-class demand to the present time through a rising private debt, whose service has increasingly undermined the disposable income of wage earners. Hence, the neoliberal reproduction schema had an expiration date from the outset.

The "added value" of the reproduction schema we present is to show the multiplier effect of glw-surplus value on production, investment, wage and employment, and on the other hand the corrosive impact of interest-bearing capital on economic equilibrium. A redistribution of income in favour of wage labour at the expense of interest-bearing capital would have a positive effect on the economy and could, under certain circumstances, contribute to the normalisation of the economic situation. Nevertheless, such redistribution impinges on the balance of power between capital and wage labour and, more specifically, on the dominance of money capital and the erosion of the bargaining power of labour over the last decades through the so-called globalisation, an erosion that now the most official monetary institutions recognise. For example, the Bank for International Settlements, in its recent annual report (Bank for International Settlements, 2017), explicitly admits this erosion, which it attributes to "globalisation" and "new technology".

Marx's reproduction schemas identify the necessary "proportions" between the three functional forms of capital. These "proportions" are determined through the balance of supply and demand between the two major productive departments. However, the reproduction schemas raise a central question: Who forces the capitalists to follow a specific reproduction schema? Nobody, says the French economist Alain Lipietz. A specific reproduction schema is only followed because of the regulatory framework or the "mode of regulation" that is prevalent:

> In mathematical terms, a regime of accumulation can be described as a schema of reproduction [....]. There is of course no reason why all individual capitals should come peacefully together within a coherent schema of reproduction. The regime of accumulation must therefore be materialised in the shape of norms, habits, laws and regulating networks which ensure the unity of the process and which guarantee that its agents conform more or less to the schema of reproduction in their day-to-day behaviour and struggles (both the economic struggle between capitalists and wage-earners, and that between capitals).
>
> The set of internalised rules and social procedures which incorporate social elements into individual behaviour (and one might be able to mobilise Bourdieu's concept of Habitus here) is referred as a *mode of regulation*. (Lipietz, 1987, pp. 14–15)

The neoliberal "mode of regulation", however, was based on a mistaken assumption that was upgraded to a "religious dogma": "Markets are capable of self-regulation." In other words, better regulation is institutional deregulation and poor monetary supervision.

In retrospect, when the financial crisis erupted, the distinguished neoliberal economist Alan Greenspan, who had been head of the Federal Reserve (Fed) in the critical years before the crisis, was forced to admit both the ideological content of his economic vision and his inability to understand the crisis. On 23 October 2008, in his testimony before the Committee on Oversight and Government Reform, US House of Representatives, he said:

> "I do have an ideology. My judgment is that free, competitive markets are by far the unrivaled way to organize economies. We've tried regulation. None meaningfully worked."
>
> "I made a mistake in presuming that the self-interests of organizations, specifically banks and others, were such that they were best capable of protecting their own shareholders and their equity in the firms."
>
> "I found a flaw in the model that I perceived is the critical functioning structure that defines how the world works, so to speak."
>
> "As I wrote last March, those of us who have looked to the self-interest of lending institutions to protect shareholders equity, myself especially, are

in a state of shocked disbelief." (Committee on Oversight and Government Reform, 2008, pp. 15–16, 14–15, 16, 8 respectively)

Nevertheless, deregulation was much more than a "mistake". As we will show by examining the crisis in its financial dimension, the deregulated financial system was not only the Achilles' heel of the global economic system, but also a necessary part of the neoliberal reproduction schema. The "bubble" is definitely indispensable in order to create the necessary conditions that allow the system, for a while, to be compatible with "social reproduction".

NOTES

1. OECD definition: "Net household saving is defined as the subtraction of household consumption expenditure from household disposable income, plus the change in net equity of households in pension funds" (https://data.oecd.org/hha/household-savings.htm).
2. OECD definition: "Real household net disposable income is defined as the sum of household final consumption expenditure and savings, minus the change in net equity of households in pension funds. This indicator also corresponds to the sum of wages and salaries, mixed income, net property income, net current transfers and social benefits other than social transfers in kind, less taxes on income and wealth and social security contributions paid by employees, the self-employed and the unemployed" (https://data.oecd.org/hha/household-disposable-income.htm).

BIBLIOGRAPHY

Bank for International Settlements. (2017). *87th Annual Report, 1st April 2016–31st March 2017*. Basel. Retrieved from: https://www.bis.org/publ/arpdf/ar2017e.pdf

Committee on Oversight and Government Reform. (2008, October 23). *The Financial Crisis and the Role of Federal Regulators*. Retrieved from: https://www.gpo.gov/fdsys/pkg/CHRG-110hhrg55764/html/CHRG-110hhrg55764.htm

Dew-Becker, I., & Cordon R. J. (2005, September). *Where did the Productivity Growth Go? Inflation Dynamics and the Distribution of Income*. Retrieved from: http://zfacts.com/metaPage/lib/gordon-Dew-Becker.pdf

Lipietz, A. (1987). *Mirages and Miracles: the Crises of Global Fordism*. London, New York: Verso.

Marx, K. (1992). *Capital: A Critique of Political Economy*. Volume Two. London, New York: Penguin Books.

Tombazos, S. (2014). *Time in Marx. The Categories of Time in Marx's Capital*. Leiden, Boston: Brill Academic Publisher.

CHAPTER 4

Money Capital, Fictitious Capital and "Toxic" Capital

Abstract Money capital, as a seemingly autonomous entity, does not produce value. Its "profit" arises as interest and dividend from industrial profit for productively invested loans, as interest on taxes levied by the state to service the public debt and as interest from wages for consumer loans to workers. Money capital corresponds to a real value that is either productively invested or consumed privately, but which can expand fictitiously, thus creating a "toxic value". Financial derivatives created an opaque environment and permitted an unprecedented growth of fictitious value and of its "toxic part". They stimulated consumption and investment for a while, but they also led to an unsustainable growth of debt that was an integral part of neoliberal schemas of accumulation.

Keywords Financial derivatives • Opacity of financial system • Fictitious value • "Toxic value"

The failure of supervisors to predict the coming crisis is not only due to the ideological nature of their economic approach nor to a "flaw in the model" that "defines how the world works". It is also due to the real opacity that the deregulation of the financial system has caused. The financial derivative products obfuscate reality to such an extent that every attempt at a scientific understanding easily degenerated into a kind of metaphysical geometry, in which even the squaring of the circle seemed feasible. More

© The Author(s) 2019   45
S. Tombazos, *Global Crisis and Reproduction of Capital*, Palgrave
Insights into Apocalypse Economics,
https://doi.org/10.1007/978-3-030-05725-1_4

specifically, the dominant (highly mathematical but ultimately metaphysical) approach's fragmentary understanding of reality led to the illusion that the shifting around of financial risk was tantamount to its disappearance. The crisis began when the precariousness of a large part of US mortgages was revealed.

In the framework of "financial innovation" and "risk management", investment banks were able to mix loans in order to create financial derivative products, which could be sold on the markets. The most well-known financial derivatives of this type were Mortgage-Backed Securities (MBS) and Collateralized Debt Obligations (CDO): Private investment banks granted or bought loans from the original lending institution for the purchase of real estate in order to convert them into securities and sell them in this form.

They considered that the selling of these financial derivatives was an efficient way of avoiding the risk of potential Non-Performing Loans (NPL). In theory, the risk was in this way transferred to the buyers of these financial derivatives, that is, mainly to hedge funds, pension funds, insurance companies and other banks. These buyers appropriated a large part of the interest of the loans of which the securities were composed, and the sellers (the investment banks) earned fees for their services (collecting and transferring the interest to the buyers). In this way, the risk of NPLs spread globally in a myriad of investors and portfolios and was thus considered reasonable.

The hedge funds often used to create new financial derivatives backed on the initial securities that they bought, that is, they created financial derivatives to the power of two, and with them the opacity of the global finance was more and more dense.

In the 2000s, before the crisis, the mortgage credit transformed by the investment banks into securities was significantly expanded depending on its quality. It is worth mentioning that, while the state-sponsored Fannie Mae and Freddie Mac in the USA granted and securitised "prime mortgage loans", the private investment banks securitised the most risky loans, the so-called subprime loans.

This is why the expansion of securitised mortgage credit by private investment banks is so important. It essentially brought about a radical change in the philosophy of the financial system. From a system where the granting of a loan meant the assumption of the underlying risk, we moved to a system that seemingly dissociates the loan from the risk through the sale of the loan in the form of a financial derivative. The quality of the loan was increasingly of less interest to the banker, but its quantity interested them more and more.

Of course, several subdivisions of MBS, CDO and others securities were created, based on the estimation of their underlying risk. A crucial role in this stratification was played by the various rating agencies. The best securities, rated AAA, were the first category, the so-called super senior. The second category of AA and A rated securities was named "senior", the third with a BBB rating and BB "mezzanine" up to the last category without a rating called "equity". The markets also used to call the financial derivatives of this last category "toxic waste". The latter, as long as they did not release their "toxicity", that is as long as the NPLs were very limited, were also the most profitable.

This last category of financial derivatives was supposed to protect the other categories by acting as an "alarm". Since these "toxic" securities would collapse first, there would be enough time to react in order to protect the value of the better ones. However, the rating agencies, a large part of whose profits came from the rating of such securities, had a strong incentive to rate them very "generously". This is why, even the "AAA securities", as revealed later during the crisis, were not always much less "toxic" as the "equity" ones. The rating agencies were supposed to be "neutral observers" of the financial activities, but in reality they were part of them.

The rating agencies, especially Moody's Investors Service, Standard & Poor's (S&P) and Fitch Ratings that control approximately 95% of the market, not only are responsible for the crisis in the derivative markets, but today play a crucial role as a "surveillance and punishment mechanism", as M. Foucault would say, against governments that do not strictly respect the neoliberal orthodoxy about fiscal policy. When they upgrade a state bond, for example, they ramp up political pressure on the state to comply with the norm. If the state does not comply, it has to pay the price: the rise of the interest rate on sovereign debt. It is worth noting that the rating agencies have never published or explained their rating methodology. Probably, if they have a methodology, they use it in a very flexible manner, that is in a political manner.

According to a study by Mian and Sufi, in the period 2001–2005, the volume of the most risky mortgage loans grew faster than that of the less risky ones (Mian & Sufi, 2008). The study presents data on loan applications rejected in the period 1996–2000 by geographical area, thus calculating the credit demand that was not satisfied. The areas that experienced the largest increase in mortgage loans in the early 2000s were precisely the areas where the rejection rates of such loans were the highest in the period

1996–2000. This is why an increase of non-performing mortgage loans has been observed since 2005. They grew from 11% of the total on 31 March 2005 to over 16% two years later, despite the relative dynamism of the US economy over the same period.

Financial derivatives of mortgage credit, such as CDO and MBS, belong to a broader category of securities called Asset-Backed Securities (ABS). Securitised business loans, consumer loans, commercial loans, credit cart overdrafts and so forth increased from the early 1980s, and especially from 1990. While in 1980 the value of these ABSs did not exceed a few tens of billions of dollars, in 1993 it exceeded 2000 billion, and in 2006 it approached 11000 billion (Moati, November 2008).

And of course, as long as the volume of the loans, whether securitised or not, kept growing, private debt kept increasing too. While the US household savings rate followed a downward trend until the major crisis erupted, household debt followed an upward trend. From less than 5000 billion dollars in 1995, it reached 13975 billion dollars in 2008. At the same time, the debt of non-financial corporations grew from less than 3000 to 7027 billion, federal government debt from around 3500 to 5274 billion—despite its downward trend until 2002—and the debt of states and local authorities grew from about 1000 to 2222 billion (Moati, November 2008).

Investment banks, less tightly supervised than commercial banks, completely circumvented supervisory authorities and rules by placing their financial derivative activities in off-balance-sheet entities. These off-balance-sheet activities are essentially equivalent to a parallel and fully deregulated banking system, based on the so-called Special Purpose Vehicles (SPV) or Special Investment Vehicles (SIV) that served as legal cover for the investment banks. The SPVs or SIVs funded the securities they issued by creating short-term debt (e.g. in order to grant a loan or to buy mortgage loans from the original lender), with an amount of Asset-Backed Commercial Paper (ABCP) and, finally, with own capital funds that were, as a general rule, a small part of total funding (often below 2% or even 1%). The SPVs and SIVs record as assets the notional values of the various MBSs, CDOs and other ABSs titles they issue (Down, 2007), but since these financial derivatives are not sold at their notional value and losses are recorded, the leverage, which is inversely proportional to the part of their own capital in the total "investment", is enormous. Their own capital is lost, ABCP value abruptly shrinks and only a huge amount of indebtedness remains (Aglietta, 2008).

After the collapse of Lehman Brothers, it was obvious that the Credit Default Swap (CDS) market would also enter in the vicious circle of the crisis. CDSs are another major category of financial derivatives. The CDS market operates as follows: Financial institutions, especially investment banks and big insurance companies, issue CDS securities for granted loans that are supposed to cover the lenders against the risk of their lending. Like vehicle insurance, which distributes the cost for repairing damages to all insured vehicle owners, CDSs are supposed to distribute risk and losses to CDS owners, who essentially swap with each other the risk and losses of their lending. Beyond its opacity, this market has a very uncommon peculiarity for an insurance business. There is no vehicle insurance company that covers a 10,000-dollar car for damages above this value (e.g. 20,000 dollars). And, of course, one cannot insure a car one does not own (e.g. the car of one's neighbour). CDSs, while allegedly insuring creditors against borrowers who may not be able to service their debt, may insure for much larger amounts than the granted credit. It is also possible to buy CDSs for a debt without being the lending institution for this particular debt. Some hedge funds, for example, bought and sold (in the secondary markets) CDSs on Greek sovereign debt without holding any Greek sovereign bonds. In other words, these securities, although considered as a kind of "insurance", are themselves governed by the logic of the "casino economy" (Chavagneux, 2008). When Lehman collapsed, the financial institutions that issued CDSs for its debt, more accurately for a much higher value than Lehman's debt, needed the state to rescue them.

As in any chaotic system, in this financial chaos a small or even subtle change can have enormous repercussions. When the Federal Reserve (Fed) increased its key interest rate by 0.25%, nothing unusual and nothing important happened. However, on the other side of the lending-borrowing chain, the borrowers who could barely service their debt in 2005 could not service it any more in 2007, after the much more significant increase in the interest rate on their mortgage or consumer debt. And because the growth of NPLs leads to increased supply in the real estate market, the bubble (Soros, 2008) of property values was deflated, and along with this bubble, on which a whole world of credit pyramids, CDSs, derivative products and securities of all kinds was based ..., an entire world of fictitious values collapsed. The crisis was officially recognised since the central banks were forced to restore the liquidity (with public money) of the private financial system: on 9 August 2007.

The neoliberal economists used to present the financial derivatives as a rational management of financial risk. Their common methodological flaw was to implicitly consider the individual risk management as equal to social risk management. However, what seems to constitute for a private corporation or credit institution "rational management" can be irrational, irresponsible or even catastrophic for society. The original lenders transfer the risk to the investment banks that buy the loans to sell them in the form of financial derivatives. The hedge funds and other institutional investors who buy these securities sell them to other investors in their original form or in the form of new financial derivatives backed by the former and so on. This continuous shifting of risk to the Generalised Other, instead of being rational risk management, transforms this risk from individual to social, from private to systemic, from local to national and global. The Generalised Other is all of us, that is the global system.

Of course, methodological individualism is not just an epistemological error. It covers material interests of the dominant class, even if it does not result from a conscious act, but from the "systemic blindness" that Marx analyses in the framework of the "fetishism of the commodity".

The way in which the deregulated financial system functioned did not only lead to an unprecedented crisis of the financial system itself. It also led to a profound crisis of the reproduction schemas of capital. The deregulated financial system was an integral part of neoliberal economic growth. The bubbles on which this growth was based were the necessary price to pay for maintaining the rhythm of accumulation (although slow in comparison to the valorisation rhythm), which was too fast in comparison to a sustainable rhythm of realisation of value resulting from the neoliberal income distribution.

The deregulated financial system created a "constructively" chaotic schema of reproduction because it created relatively favourable conditions for realising value but simultaneously undermined the foundations on which it was based. The financial system became increasingly sensitive to minor changes, such as a slight increase in the key interest rates of central banks or an apparently insignificant fall in real estate prices.

The fall in real estate prices was a possibility that the specialised econometric models excluded from the beginning, because their predictions were generally based on the data of the last 20 years only, in which no downward trend in property prices was registered. As Alan Greenspan said in 2008, a "Nobel Prize was awarded for discovery of the pricing model that underpins much of the advance in derivatives markets. This modern risk management paradigm held sway for decades. The whole intellectual edifice, however, collapsed in the summer of last year, because the data inputted into the risk management models generally covered only the last two decades, a period of euphoria" (Committee on Oversight and Government Reform, 2008, p. 9).

These risky "risk management models" in the real estate market were, however, responsible to a large extent for the credit expansion in not only this market but also in the automobile market and in the consumer goods market more generally. When the price of property increases, the same collateral can theoretically be pledged for another credit for another purpose. This is the reason why the crisis in the real estate market derivatives led to a crisis in all derivatives markets: The financial derivatives were interrelated.

In order to better understand how the financial system is structured by exploitative practices, how it is an organic part of the neoliberal reproduction schema, Marx's analysis of money capital is indispensable.

Money capital is part of industrial capital according to Marx, not an independent entity. From the point of view of the owner of money capital, however, the money (m) which he lent to the industrialist appears to exhibit the "(meta)physical" property to multiply itself over time. It is enough to deposit his money in an interest-bearing bank account to multiply it: m is converted into m' because interest is added to it. In fact, however, the lender's m, to "generate" interest, must be transferred to the "active" capitalist through the banking system, who will productively invest it together with his own capital in monetary form. In other words, m is only part of M in industrial capital circuits. And, of course, interest is only part of industrial profit or surplus value.

The same applies to the owner of money buying shares from the industrialist. He exchanges his money against a title of ownership over the total industrial capital, and earns a right to a share of the industrial profit: the dividend. The latter, like interest, is not something different from industrial profit, but is only a part of it. For Marx, industrial profit includes all the subdivisions of surplus value, all of its "faces": profit remaining in the productive business after interest and dividends payments, interest and dividend. The sale of new shares in the stock market (primary market) is essentially direct borrowing, while borrowing through the bank system is indirect borrowing, because the bank acts as a mediator between the lender and the borrower.

Hence, for Marx, there is no large or small amount of money capital compared to industrial capital. There is only a large or small part of industrial capital that appears simultaneously as "independent" money capital, which is also recorded in a second accounting book since it belongs to another capitalist: the owner of shares or interest-bearing capital.

From the point of view of the industrialist, industrial profit has three destinations: private consumption, productive investment and nonproductive investment (in shares, in a bank interest-bearing account, etc.). However, the economy is a system. And, of course, the individual point of view does not necessarily coincide with "theory" in the ancient Greek meaning of this term: seeing the whole "picture", that is, having a global view, in order to understand how a system works. Industrial profit has only two destinations: productive investment and consumption. When the industrialist A saves part of his profit in the bank, the bank lends this money, for example, to industrialist B, who will invest it productively in his own industry. When industrialist A buys shares of industry B in the primary market (a new share issuance of industry B), he gives money to industrialist B who will invest it in his own industry if he aims to increase "his" industrial profit: Industrialist B has to pay a dividend to industrial A, which is part of the industrial profit of his own industry.

If industrialist A buys shares from industrialist B or from any other industrialist in the secondary market, that is, if he "invests" money into the stock market, someone else will sell these shares. The same amount of money that enters into the secondary stock market (and generally securities markets) from one door goes out from the other, because when one buys the other sells. Of course, to the extent that speculators sell shares to buy other shares, part of the money in circulation is "trapped" in the secondary markets, where it can only contribute to the increase of fictitious values. As Rudolf Hilferding already understood very well, speculation not only does not create any value but it does not generate any profit either: Speculation is a zero-sum game. Speculation in the secondary markets is not different in its principle from betting in horse racing:

> The different valuations made by buyers and sellers, at a particular time, results in losses for some speculators and gains for others. The profit of one is other's loss; and this is in sharp contrast with the profit of the productive capitalist; for the profit of the capitalist class is not a loss for the working class, which cannot expect, under normal capitalist conditions, to receive more than the value of its labour force. (Hilferding, 1981, p. 136)

From the point of view of the securities purchaser and the lender, the process of valorisation of value is simplified to m-m'. In the phantasmagoria of stock markets and banks, money acquires the capacity to multiply itself by magic. In this metaphysical world of "parthenogenesis", that is the creation of value without the mediation of human labour or the consumption of labour power, thrives what Marx calls "fictitious capital" (Chesnais, 2016).

According to Marx, fictitious capital is every capital that appears as an asset in more than one accounting book. A share is by definition fictitious capital because it appears from the outset as an independent value from the industrial capital that corresponds to it.

However, while the shares issued and sold by the industrialist originally correspond (more or less) to a real capital, despite already representing a fictitious value because they appear as assets twice, the buying and selling of shares in secondary markets leads to a relative "autonomization" of their value vis-à-vis the real capital they correspond to and often to a fictitious value to the power of two. Because some speculators think that they can sell some shares at a higher price than they can buy them, they are willing to buy them at a price higher than the value of the real capital they correspond to. Besides, speculators do not really know the value of the real capital that these shares represent; they only estimate it. The increase in demand for these shares leads to the rise in their price, and along with their price the fictitious value to the power of two of all portfolios that include them also rises.

Theoretically, it is possible for the shareholders or securities owners to fictitiously enrich themselves when the market price of their shares/securities increases. In times of economic euphoria, while GDP grows by 2% or 3%, the fictitious value of several shares or securities may increase by 15% or 20% per annum. But this fictitious wealth to the power of two vanishes as soon as its owners decide massively to turn it into real money buying real commodities. Because the supply rises sharply in comparison to the demand for these shares/securities, their prices collapse and the fictitious wealth evaporates with the same ease with which it had been created. Due to the mimetism that prevails in market behaviour, the fictitious value of shares/securities is subject to sharp cyclical fluctuations: It inflates and deflates (often below the real value), depending on the expectation of returns that determine supply and demand.

Nevertheless, fictitious capital affects the so-called real economy through the so-called wealth effect, especially when it goes beyond the real value that it is supposed to represent. When it swells, it leads to decisions that have, for example, an impact on private consumption: An average income household of self-employed, who see the fictitious value of its shares or securities growing, prefer sometimes to borrow to consume in order not to lose the "profit" promised by this fictitious increase in the value of its shares or securities.

Marx's analysis of interest-bearing capital, and more generally of money capital as a seemingly independent form, emphasises the credit mechanisms linking capitalists to one another. However, in our times, and more specifically in the neoliberal era, there is another form of money capital that is very important for understanding the present crisis. When money capital is used as credit extended to wage earners, the interest is not any more a part of industrial profit or surplus value, but a part of the wage. In this case, money capital, through credit, leads to the growth of the purchasing power of wage labour in the present time, but reduces (to a greater extent, unless the real interest rate is zero or negative) its future purchasing power, because the wage earner has to service his debt. This is tantamount to an increase in capitalist income through debt servicing. To the surplus value produced in the process of exploitation of labour power is added the interest. To the exploitation rate, the interest rate is added as a kind of "direct exploitation" (Lapavitsas, 2013), which is not mediated by the productive consumption of labour power. The interest-bearing capital seems in this case to facilitate the reproduction of labour power in the present time independently of its reproduction in the future.

In other words, because in the neoliberal times the exploitation rate of the working class is increasing on the one hand, while a share of the total surplus value is "liberated" to be used as credit to the working class on the other, the social surplus product is not only the surplus value through the exploitation of labour power in the production process of capital, but also the interest through the "investment" of money capital in the reproduction process of labour power itself.

However, when the accumulation of rights over future wages, in the form of ABS or classic loans, cannot be redeemed due to unsustainable debt or NPLs and the collaterals of these loans are not sufficient, then these rights are fictitious rights to the power of two, or, according to market terminology, they are "toxic capitals": Not only they are fictitious because of their seemingly autonomous life, but a part of them does not represent any real value.

States, through their interventions in order to rescue the financial system, essentially undertake to rescue these fictitious values or "toxic capitals" by transferring the cost to the taxpayer as much as possible. The degree of "toxicity" of these values, however, is not really known in advance. It becomes itself a matter of class struggle. The so-called welfare state is more and more dismantled and the impoverished social strata grow, because this is the only way to reduce the "toxicity" of the accumulated rights over future wages.

Neoliberalism is actually a very "flexible" ideology in its principles. The same famous mainstream economists, who believed that the self-interest of financial institutions "were best capable of protecting their shareholders and equity in the firms", did not hesitate at all to urge governments to orchestrate public rescues of these same shareholders and equity. These financial institutions were much too big to fail (and it was not the first time, and certainly not the last). As Alan Greenspan said in 2008:

> to avoid severe retrenchment, banks and other financial intermediaries will need the support that only the substitution of sovereign credit for private credit can bestow. The $700 billion Troubled Assets Relief Program is adequate to serve that need. (Committee on Oversight and Government Reform, 2008, p. 8)

The 700-billion-dollar assets were, of course, only the first stage of the public rescue of banks and other financial intermediaries. In the past ten years, the cost of this rescue is not counted in billions of dollars, but in many trillions, as we will see in the next chapter.

As the recent Greek experience shows, holding government debt can itself prove to be "toxic": When the state is unable to service its debt, what else can the possession of sovereign debt that cannot be serviced amount to if not the possession of fictitious value to the power of two? The "haircut" of sovereign debt simply means that the fictitious nature of a part of the value of government bonds is socially recognised as such and written off.

A government bond is a right over future taxation, that is, a right over future gross wage and future gross capitalist income. One could say that a bond is fictitious capital to the power of two right from the beginning because its only "real" collateral is the presumed solvency of the state. Nevertheless, political power is often more "real" than material collaterals. During the neoliberal period, government bonds increasingly represent a right over future wages and decreasingly over future capitalist income. To a large extent, this is due to the fact that "globalisation" creates tax competition amongst states, which, in order to attract foreign capital, reduce capital taxation and increase labour taxation. Capital migrates much more easily (and without a passport or need of residence permission) than labour. Capitalists who save money because of these neoliberal taxation policies can convert it in government bonds in order to claim a share of future taxation.

As we will see in the next chapter, the value of government bonds (and of other securities) was "rescued" with an unprecedented intervention by central banks in primary and secondary markets. What else can this intervention mean, than that sovereign debt in the USA, the EU-15, the Eurozone and Japan was unsustainable, and should be haircut on the basis of social criteria? It is possible to haircut the value of the sovereign debt held by hedge funds and banks, which is not just unsustainable but also illegitimate, if not, in some cases, illegal (Chesnais, 2011), and not the sovereign debt held by pension funds. Among other things, unsustainable sovereign debt comes from the reduction in capital taxation in the name of "unhindered" global competition, the same competition that led to the current crisis and the accumulation of social ruins.

The impressive rise of fictitious capital in recent decades is also due to the increase in public debt, but it is mainly due to the growth of other forms of money capital (financial derivatives of all kinds, interest-bearing capital, shares, etc.). The same money capital appears with multiple faces, that is, it appears in multiple accounting books. When, for example, a hedge fund manufactures a financial derivative product backed by another financial derivative, that is, a fictitious capital backed by another fictitious capital, the original asset seems to be multiplied. It is an asset for the bank that granted loans through the credit card overdraft of its clients; it is an ABS asset in the accounting book of the hedge fund that bought these loans; and the CDS issued by another investment bank is an asset, which the hedge fund buys to cover its ABS derivatives. This is why in 1980 the assets of money capital were roughly equal to world GDP, while in 2010 they were four times as high (Chesnais, 2013).

The development of finance with the deregulation of the financial system in recent decades has played a double role at the three poles of the global economy:

Firstly, through the increased mobility of money capital and the more intense competition that has emerged from it, real wage growth has decelerated in favour of profit. Money capital moves towards the most profitable activities, thus imposing a "productive discipline" that requires high profit rates. This has shrunk the activities considered satisfactorily profitable and left unmet social needs evolving throughout the post-war period in the service sector (health, education, etc.), that is to say to a less dynamic sector in terms of productivity growth and hence profit growth (Husson, 2008).

Secondly, money capital offset for a while the negative impact of the downward trend of the adjusted wage share of GDP on private consumption, through the increased private consumption of households that benefitted from a greater share of interest and dividends in industrial profits and the increase in private consumption of wage labour based on borrowing. In this way, by overcoming the problem of the "realisation of value" that neoliberal capitalism itself created and managed, capital accumulation and GDP continued to grow, albeit at rates much lower than during the "golden" post-war period.

High incomes accumulate property (real estate, land, stocks, securities of all kinds), reversing the ownership relations of the upward stage of the post-war cycle. Flow or annual profit is converted into property stock. Unprecedented inequalities in income lead to unprecedented inequalities in wealth. The development of financial capital on the one hand and the rise of inequalities on the other—inequalities at all levels of social life: not only income and material wealth, but also health and life expectancy, education, exposure to ecological risk, quality of free time—are the two sides of the same coin.

However, increasing wealth inequalities enabled long-term economic growth before the crisis for a very simple reason: The debt service of households and their private consumption in general can also be ensured by the selling of property. In this case, the latter has an impact on private consumption, just as an upward trend has in the savings rate. The loan is not usually annual but long-term (2 + 28 or 3 + 27 for mortgages, i.e. during the first two or three years of the loan's 30-year service period, the borrower does not fully service the debt).

The fact that social inequalities developed alongside money capital does not relieve industrial capital of any responsibility. The concept of "money capital" is largely a mental abstraction. In fact, there is rarely money capital and industrial capital in their pure form. Money capital is mostly the way in which industrial capital is "socialised", that is, the way in which individual capitalist ownership of the means of production is transformed into the collective property of the capitalist class. If one opens the accounting book of an industrialist, he will find there a number of shares of other industries, commercial enterprises, investment funds, banks and so forth.

If one tries to find out to whom the material capital managed by the industrialist himself really belongs to, he will discover that it belongs not only to the latter but also to a number of other capitalists: other industrialists, traders, investment funds, banks, insurance companies and so forth. Sometimes, it even belongs—to a lesser extent—to his own workers who bought some shares in his industry. The fact that even wage earners often have a relatively small number of shares or other securities contributes to the ideological confusion that can be observed in our time, a confusion that neoliberal ideology preserves and cultivates.

Therefore, it is a mistake to explain the growing divergence between the rate of profit and the rate of accumulation, or the increase in the ratio Surplus Value/Net Investment, through the increase of the share of surplus value appropriated by money capital. The productive capitalist invests less and less in productive activities because there are no new productive activities that promise an "acceptable" rate of profit. This is why he invests a large share of "his" surplus value in other industries' shares, in bank shares, in investment funds and so forth. The rise of interests and dividends as a share of surplus value is the symptom and not the cause of the above-mentioned divergence. The fact that the share of surplus value that the productive enterprise maintains after interest and dividend payments evolves alongside accumulation (Duménil & Lévy, 2011), does not change in any way the reasons that lead to this divergence: The same industrialist who pays interest and dividends also receives interest and dividends, because he had chosen in the first place to invest in his productive industry less surplus value in order to invest another part of this surplus value as money capital.

The narrative about the development of money capital (or of "finance" in more general terms) is an abstract narrative. At a more concrete level of analysis, one can say that a greater degree of interpenetration of productive and money capital prevails today. In 1910, R. Hilferding named this interpenetration of money capital (*Geldkapital*) and industrial capital as "finance capital" (*Finanzkapital*). However, the finance capital of his time was the result of the interpenetration of industrial capital and banks. In our days, bank capital is one of the components of a multifarious money capital, including relatively new institutions such as investment funds, insurances and pension funds. In our days, finance capital results from the union of industrial capital and this multifarious money capital.

This is why, today, more than in the past, every "financial crisis" will affect the "real economy". In 2007–2008, the "financial system" did not collapse on its own. It was a whole schema of reproduction based on the divorce of economic progress in the narrow sense and social progress that collapsed, a schema of social inequality production.

Of course, the economic policies of the states and the central banks have saved the system. The question is whether these policies have affected the neoliberal schema of reproduction in a way that would ensure a short- or long-term growth period without major recessions.

BIBLIOGRAPHY

Aglietta, M. (2008, February). Comprendre la crise du crédit structuré. *La lettre du CEPII*, 275. Retrieved from: http://www.cepii.fr/francgraph/pageperso/aglietta.htm

Chavagneux, C. (2008, November). Comment les États ont sauvé le capitalisme. *Alternatives économiques*, 274.

Chesnais, F. (2011). *Les dettes illégitimes: Quand les banques font main basse sur les politiques publiques*. Paris: Raisons d'agir.

Chesnais, F. (2013). The first five years of the on-going world economic and financial crisis. *Social Sciences: Trilingual Revue of Social Research*, Volume 2–3, 148–162.

Chesnais, F. (2016). *Finance Capital Today. Corporations and Banks in the Lasting Global Slump*. Leiden-Boston: Brill Academic Publisher.

Committee on Oversight and Government Reform (2008, October 23). *The Financial Crisis and the Role of Federal Regulators*. Retrieved from: https://www.gpo.gov/fdsys/pkg/CHRG-110hhrg55764/html/CHRG-110hhrg55764.htm

Down R. (2007, July 26). CDOs: Toxic or Tonic. *HSBC Global Research*.

Duménil, G., & Lévy, D. (2011). *The Crisis of Neoliberalism*. Cambridge, MA: Harvard University Press.

Hilferding, R. (1981). *Finance capital: A study of the latest phase of capitalist development*. London, Boston and Henley: Routledge & Kegan Paul.

Husson, M. (2008). *Un pur capitalisme*. Lausanne: Éd. Page deux.

Lapavitsas, K. (2013). *Profiting without Producing. How Finance Exploits Us All*. London: Verso.

Mian, A., & Sufi A. (2008, January). *The Consequences of Mortgage Credit Expansion: Evidence from the 2007 Mortgage Crisis*. Retrieved from: https://www.moodys.com/microsites/crc2008/papers/cons_morg_cred_exp.pdf

Moatti, S. (2008, November). La machine à dette. *Alternatives économiques*, 274.

Soros, G. (2008). *The New Paradigm for Financial Markets: The Credit Crisis of 2008 and What it Means*. New York: The Perseus Books Group.

CHAPTER 5

Economic Policies and Economic Perspectives

Abstract Economic policies prevented the collapse of the financial system and in Europe saved the euro, but they did not lead to an exit from the crisis. The main pillar of monetary policy was negative real interest rates by central banks, but these have a number of "side effects" that require central banks to shift course. However, moving from the state of an unprecedentedly prolonged monetary "emergency" to a state of normality is not an easy task. It would also adversely affect fiscal policies because it would lead to higher interest rates on public debt. The austerity policies in southern Europe establish conditions that no longer allow the return to growth rates of the initial euro period. Greece has been transformed into a debt colony.

Keywords "Quantitative easing" • Fiscal policy • Public debt • Key interest rate • Crisis in South European countries

The current historical crisis is not a crisis stemming from the "tendency of the rate of profit to fall". Even authors who generally argue in favour of this interpretation of the crisis, like M. Roberts and R. Brenner (Brenner, 2016), do not really show a fall in the rate of profit in the neoliberal period in comparison to the 1970s. M. Roberts, for example, writes (and presents data to support his view):

© The Author(s) 2019
S. Tombazos, *Global Crisis and Reproduction of Capital*, Palgrave
Insights into Apocalypse Economics,
https://doi.org/10.1007/978-3-030-05725-1_5

In the G7 economies, the rate of profit fell secularly between 1950 and 2011 because in that period, the organic composition of capital rose much more than did the rate of surplus value [...]. But in the neoliberal period, when profitability rose, organic composition actually fell slightly while the surplus value rose significantly. (Roberts, 2016, pp. 223–224)

In his figure 12.1 (Roberts, 2016, p. 224) that shows the rate of profit (simple mean average) in 14 countries, one can see a slight fall in the rate from the end of the 1990s to the beginning of the 2000s and a rise between 2002 and 2007. How can one explain the current historic crisis as a direct result of the law of the tendency of the rate of profit to fall? One has to explain why in a moment in which the counter-tendencies to the fall of the rate of profit prevail, one of the most severe crises in capitalist history breaks out.

Of course, on the other hand, the current crisis is not unrelated to the fall of the rate of profit in the 1970s. The current crisis derives from the policies implemented to deal with the fall of profitability in the 1970s. This decline in profitability inaugurated a long-term downward wave. An attempt was made to overcome it by changing the capital-labour balance of forces in favour of capital. The current crisis is the crisis of the neoliberal response to the downward wave, as the goal of changing the capital-labour balance of forces was successful and the profit rate rose again.

The neoliberal capitalism that results from the application of the new policies could present an image of precarious recovery (with low rate of accumulation and GDP growth) at the cost of a continuous expansion of social inequalities and poverty. For instance, income inequality in the USA in 2006 was even greater than that in 1928, and throughout the period from 1928 to 2006, it had never reached such levels: the 10% of the higher-income earners earning 50% of GDP in 2006 against 48% in 1928. It is not a coincidence that during the whole period from 1917 to 2006 (Piketty & Saez, 2008), the two peaks of income inequality were observed shortly before the crisis of 1929–1933 and that of 2007 onwards. It is worth mentioning that the developed countries with the lowest rates of unemployment, like the USA, Britain or Ireland, had the highest poverty rates, as defined by the United Nations Human Development Reports. This simply means that a significant number of people were not registered in the unemployment statistics for various reasons, including the high rate of people in the prison in the USA in comparison to that of a country like France (high rate of unemployment, low rate of prison population).

Neoliberal capitalism was able to present this image of precarious recovery as long as it could mitigate the impact of social inequalities on the schema of reproduction by developing the "virtues" of a new and ultramodern version of "voodoo": deregulated finance and financial derivatives of all kinds.

In the EU, and especially in the Eurozone, this transfer of surplus value transformed in loanable money capital, beyond its class dimension, was also complicated by a national dimension. The countries of northern Europe lent money to the countries of southern Europe (Husson, 2013).

Without any doubt, the adoption of the euro was a terrible idea, as it created an incomplete monetary union. However, this union seemed, before the crisis, to have a positive impact on the Euro area economy, as it led to a vigorous growth of GDP especially in the southern economies, as well as to the convergence of their per capita income with that of the more advanced northern economies (Tombazos, 2011).

The adoption of the euro eliminates one more protective barrier to the "unhindered" movement of goods and capital in the single monetary area, since the national currencies were abolished and could no longer be devalued to offset foreign trade deficits in the countries with current account deficits. In this framework, the European economies tended to specialise themselves even more in commodities in which they had a comparative advantage, and became more interdependent. However, the benefit of specialisation is not the same for all European economies, nor is it necessarily sustainable in the long run, because some economies are trapped in "retrograde" specialisations, that is, in specialisations that are not promising in terms of added value growth.

In the Euro area, the foreign trade deficits could only be dealt with "internal devaluation", that is with reduction in wages and profits. However, during the first period of the euro, that is before the crisis, the single currency did not lead to any internal devaluation. Because money capital was not concerned about any possible national currency devaluation, since there was no national currency to devalue, it kept financing the foreign trade deficits by transferring surplus value from countries with current account surpluses to countries with current account deficits. Hence, the external trade deficits of the less competitive economies of the southern Eurozone increased, but money capital did not really get affected. Based on the belief that the authorities would never allow the collapse of the euro or the shrinking of the Euro area, money capital continued lending the southern countries, where the ratio Private Debt/GDP and per capita income grew at a particularly fast pace.

The fact that the inflation rate was higher in the southern European countries than in the northern European countries, while the nominal interest rates were more or less the same (low real interests rates in the southern countries), created favourable conditions for private borrowing, both for enterprises and for households.

Germany's real wage stagnation in the 2000s, even before the crisis, had a negative effect on the foreign trade of the countries of the southern Eurozone. Wage stagnation in Germany increased the country's export surpluses and led to an appreciation of the euro against the dollar, making the trade of the southern euro area countries less competitive against third countries.

In fact, the euro, in its initial stage, until the crisis of 2008, created a bubble of private lending in southern Eurozone, where the growth rates of GDP and wages grew faster than those in northern Eurozone countries.

Greece is not the exception to this rule. In contrast to the legend that was cultivated during the period of memorandums, the crisis in Greece did not come from an "uncontrollable" public debt, but, as in the other southern Eurozone countries and Ireland, it came from a very fast growth of its banking system and private debt under conditions of deficient banking supervision. The dominant interpretation of the crisis attributes this to excessive sovereign debt by playing down private debt. However, the analysis of public and private debt, based on statistical data and not on ideological beliefs, reveals another reality (Truth Committee on Public Debt, 2015).

Despite the fact that the public debt in Greece was increasing in amount, it was stable as a percentage of GDP. Between 1995 and 2007, public debt fluctuated around 100% of GDP, which is a relatively high percentage in comparison to the Maastricht criterion (60%), but not so unique for a Eurozone country. It is worth reminding the reader that despite the Maastricht criterion, Italy and Belgium managed to be accepted into the Eurozone with a larger sovereign debt than Greece. In 1999, according to the data of the European Commission (European Commission, 2017), Italy's sovereign debt was 109.6% of its GDP and Belgium's was 108.2%.

It is also worth mentioning that the primary balance of the government budget, taking into account the stock-flow adjustment, was slightly positive in Greece in the period between 1992 and 2007, while budget expenditure, as a percentage of GDP, was lower than the average expenditure of the Euro area.

On the contrary, Greece's private debt since 1999, in view of the adoption of the euro, and during the euro period up to the crisis of 2008, almost doubled as a percentage of GDP. The current crisis appears initially in Greece as a crisis of its banking system that had to face the increase in Non-Performing Loans (NPL), as in the rest of southern Europe and in Ireland. The first rescue of the Greek banking system took place in 2008, before anyone even thought about a "sovereign debt" crisis.

However, the banking crisis turned into a sovereign debt crisis when the markets refused to finance the Greek government with normal interest rates, because of their new evaluation of the risk involved in financing a government facing three problems at the same time: the banking crisis, large foreign trade deficits and a sovereign debt well above the Eurozone average, at a time when even Germany needed funds to cope with its own banking crisis. Capital flows changed direction and the Greek economy collapsed. Greece was just the weakest link of the Eurozone countries.

It is almost unnecessary to say that, if one agrees with this analysis of the initial causes of the crisis, the economic policies that were imposed by the troika in Greece and in other southern European countries, and the fiscal austerity policies that were implemented without external pressure from the governments in the northern European countries, constitute the perfect recipe for deepening the crisis and the social disaster it brings.

From 2010 until today, the lenders have been dictating the economic policies that Greece has had to implement. In contrast to a widely spread myth, the Greek economy did not sink into a continuous recession because successive Greek governments failed to make the necessary "structural" reforms imposed by the lenders, but because they actually complied with the demands of the lenders. Besides, according to the Organisation for Economic Cooperation and Development (OECD) itself, Greece was the "champion" of the so-called structural reforms in the OECD countries (OECD, 2013), that is of the austerity policies.

According to the German institute for economic research Hans-Böckler, without the bloodsucking of the Greek economy through the austerity measures of the lenders, to which the Greek political and economic establishment assented and without any "structural reform", the Greek economy would have had zero growth during 2010–2014. It would not have wasted one-fourth of GDP, while the rate of public debt would have been of 8.1 percentage points less (Gechert & Rannenberg, 2015).

The austerity measures in Greece left untouched the shareholders and the lenders of the banks, while they raised unemployment in general and long-term unemployment in particular to unprecedented highs, in comparison to the past (from 7.8% in 2008 to 23.4% in 2016), as well as in comparison to the average of the EU. They also increased the rate of poverty risk beyond 35% (European Parliament, 2016).

If the crisis in Greece was really a public debt crisis, then the success of the policies can be measured by the reduction of the sovereign debt. What can one say about policies that led to its increase from 103% of GDP before the banking crisis (in 2007) to almost 180% in 2017 (and after a substantial haircut in 2012), when they were supposed to reduce it to a sustainable level?

The perspectives of the Greek economy are very well summarised by Yanis Varoufakis:

> Last week, the third bailout package did end [20/08/2018], just as the second had ended in 2015 and the first in 2012. We now have a fourth such package that differs from the past three in two unimportant ways. Instead of new loans, payments of €96.6bn that were due to begin in 2023 will be differed until after 2032, when monies must be repaid with interest on top of other large repayments. And second, instead of calling it fourth bailout, the EU has named it, triumphantly, the 'end of bail out'.
>
> Ridiculously high VAT and small business tax rates will, of course, continue, as will fresh pension cuts and new punitive income taxes for the poorest that have been scheduled for 2019. The Greek government has also committed to maintaining a long-term budget surplus target, not counting debt repayments (3.5% of national income until 2021, and 2.2% during 2022–2060) that demands permanent austerity, a target that the IMF itself gives less than 6% probability of ever being attained by any Eurozone country. (Varoufakis, 2018)

It is also worth mentioning that the Greek crisis began in 2008 as a crisis of the banking system, when the NPLs showed an upward trend. After several bailouts of Greek banks since 2008, the NPLs reached today almost 50% of the total loans. The banking crisis has never been overcome in Greece.

The crisis in Greece, the other southern European countries and Ireland reflects the problems of the Eurozone's architecture. The euro is a common currency which exposes economies of different levels of development to "pure" competition, without an adequate political system. The political integration of Eurozone countries is far behind their economic integration. If one wants to fix permanently the exchange rate of national currencies in a monetary union, it does not merely suffice to abolish the national currencies. One must also develop policies and mechanisms that would make the new currency functional and sustainable.

The austerity policies in southern Europe during the last years brought about change in the long-term the balance of power between European countries and established conditions that no longer allow the return to growth rates of the initial euro period in the southern European countries and therefore do not favour the convergence of the Eurozone economies. Besides the fact that some elementary mechanisms for cushioning asymmetric shocks have been created, such as the European Stability Mechanism (ESM), these mechanisms simultaneously act as mechanisms of surveillance of whether or not the austerity policies are implemented by the European countries, especially if the latter are under memorandum. There is no intention to complete an incomplete monetary union that would involve, among other things, the mutualisation of public debt and the transfer of resources from the most advanced to the least advanced economies of the zone.

Paul Krugman points out that the fiscal austerity policies are socially destructive and diametrically opposed to historical experience (Krugman, 2012). Without any doubt, they are destructive but not illogical: They have some evident short-term or medium-term economic advantages and eventually some long-term geopolitical advantages for some European countries.

Let us take the case of Germany as an example. In 2010, the International Monetary Fund (IMF) suggested a "haircut" of Greek sovereign debt. The European countries (and institutions) were against it for a very simple reason. Their banks were exposed to Greek sovereign debt. For the German government, the problem was even worse not because the German banks were exposed more than the banks of other European countries (especially French banks) to Greek sovereign debt, but because Chancellor A. Merkel had already asked the German Parliament (*Bundestag*) for many hundreds of billions of euros to rescue the German banks. For her, it was politically much easier to ask for money from the *Bundestag* to rescue the "Greek people" than to ask for public money for a second rescue of the German banks (Varoufakis, 2017).

The loan granted to Greece in the framework of the First Memorandum (2010–2012) was never used to "rescue" the Greek people. It was used for paying off of the public debt that was maturing. In this way, the Greek public debt was transformed from debt held by the private sector to debt held by governments and international organisations such as the IMF. At the same time, the legal framework that regulates it changed. Greek law was gradually replaced by English law, which makes the unilateral "haircut" of the Greek public debt much more difficult.

In 2012, in the framework of the Second Memorandum, as the "haircut" of the Greek sovereign debt took place, the foreign banks were no more exposed to the Greek sovereign debt. Even the IMF recognises that:

An upfront debt restructuring would have been better for Greece although this was not acceptable to the euro partners. A delayed debt restructuring also provided a window for private creditors to reduce exposures and shift debt into official hands. (IMF, 2013, p. 28)

The German banks, like the French banks, had enough time to sell their Greek government bonds with a distant maturing day to other banks in the secondary markets. This is how the banking system in Cyprus collapsed in 2012. Through the haircut of the Greek sovereign debt, the main private banks of Cyprus lost almost 25% of the country's GDP overnight (4.5 billion euros) because they had bought Greek government bonds mainly from German and French banks between 2010 and 2012 (Tombazos, 2017). It is worth mentioning that the global crisis had not had any serious impact on Cyprus's economy before 2012.

A "haircut" on Greek sovereign debt in 2010 would have created a panic in the money markets inaugurating a sovereign debt crisis in other European countries, like Italy for example, of such dimensions that could have led to the disintegration of the Eurozone (Varoufakis, 2017). However, the management of the Greek crisis in the framework of the First Memorandum led to a very favourable interest rate on German government bonds, which were considered as more secure than other bonds of European governments, especially of southern European countries.

Austerity policies had a negative impact on the German exports to South Europe. On the other hand, Germany benefits from the immigration of highly educated people from the southern European countries. Many dozens of thousands of young Greek people, for example, educated in Greek public universities with Greek public money (e.g., engineers, doctors, informatics technicians)—professional specialisations needed in Germany—emigrated to Germany to be employed there.

On the geopolitical level, there is no doubt that the German domination in the EU and especially in the Eurozone has strengthened since 2010. For Germany, the crisis and its management was an excellent opportunity to use and to demonstrate its supremacy on the economic level, in order to strengthen its impact on the political level. It is worth mentioning that the German industrial technology development plan *Industrie* 4.0 (Forschungsunion & AKATECH, 2013; *see also* Spath, 2013) does not even mention any eventual collaboration with other European countries, while the French plan, *L'industrie du futur: Réunir la nouvelle France industrielle*, aims "to create strategic collaborations on the European and International level, especially with Germany" (Dossier de Presse, 2015, p. 13). The commercial and economic integration of Germany with the global economy, especially with the USA and China, makes the goal of European strategic collaborations of less interest. The other European countries, even France, have only to accept the German supremacy in Europe and the German strategy to become a privileged partner (as a national state dominating Europe) with the USA.

The current crisis is the result of an era in which capitalist growth is only possible through social regression. The latter had to a certain extent been hiding behind the various "bubbles" of the financial system, including the bubble of private debt in the southern Eurozone and Ireland.

As with any rule, there is an exception that confirms it. So, if we have a look at the second half of the 1990s in the USA in the relevant charts, it will be noticed that the increase in productivity went alongside the increase in real wages and in the rate of accumulation. In this economic conjuncture, many economists (even Marxists) thought that a new "golden era" was emerging. However, this deviation from the neoliberal schema in force disappeared as soon as the rate of profit began to decline again.

The initial economic "arrhythmia" of the 1970s, due to the fall in the rate of profit, was transformed into a new "arrhythmia" due to the problem of realisation of value. This change, as shown by the "golden exception" of 1996–2000 in the USA, easily regresses to the previous situation. This is why the current crisis is literally historic. Exiting the crisis cannot be achieved by deepening neoliberalism or partially revising it, a policy "summed up" by a relatively tighter supervision of the banking system.

If we look closely at the official data presented in the charts of this book, we will notice that after the great recession of 2009:

1. The rate of profit recovers to surpass the pre-crisis levels.
2. However, the level of divergence between the rate of profit and the rate of accumulation, as well as the Surplus Value/Accumulation ratio, are now, everywhere, higher than in the period before the crisis.
3. Fixed capital investment lags far behind pre-crisis levels. Since the crisis, the rate of accumulation has never reached 2% in the USA and the EU-15, while in Japan it barely exceeds 0% after a four-year disinvestment period (2009–2012). Since at least 1960, the rate of accumulation has never been so low. The tighter supervision of banks and the stabilisation of the ratio Household Debt/Disposable Income or its decline in some cases slowed down the rhythm of accumulation.

4. And, of course, labour productivity is growing at an unprecedentedly low rate at all three major poles of the advanced economies. Its growth rate is around 0.5% per year.

As it is shown in Chart 5.1, unemployment rates have fallen to pre-crisis levels, except those in the EU-15. Of course, unemployment statistics do not show the number of discouraged unemployed people.

In order to deal with the crisis, the central banks of the advanced countries carried out an unprecedented monetary experiment in economic history: They put into the economy an astronomical amount of trillions of dollars, which is reflected in the increase of the assets on their balance sheets. As a result, between 2007 and 2017 (end of the first quarter), the assets of the central banks of the advanced economies jumped from 9 trillion dollars to 25 trillion dollars. Only the three strongest central banks of the developed world (of USA, Eurozone and Japan) increased their assets from 3 trillion to 13 trillion dollars, mainly buying sovereign debt and other securities of all kinds. The Fed's assets rose from 5% of US GDP to 24%, the assets of ECB from 15% to 40% of Eurozone GDP and the assets of Bank of Japan from 21% to 90% of Japanese GDP.

Government bonds make up by far the most important share of these assets. In April 2017, the government bonds held by Fed reached 55.1% of total assets (13.4% of US public debt), the bonds held by ECB 38.8% of total assets (16.8% of Eurozone public debt) and the bonds held by Bank of Japan 84.5% of total assets (38.9% of Japanese public debt). For the Fed, the percentage of other securities (mainly debt securities of public institutions and housing loans) reached 39.8% of total assets. For the ECB

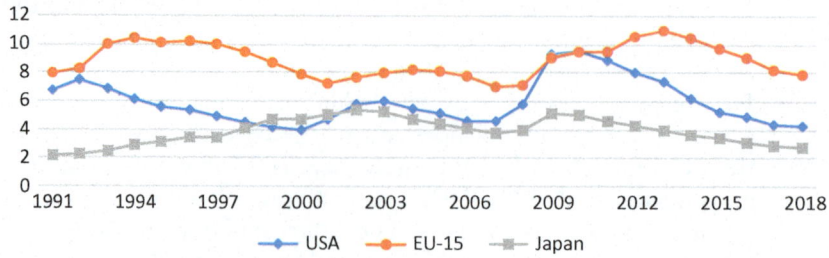

Chart 5.1 Unemployment rate in the USA, EU-15 and Japan, 1991–2018. Source: AMECO

and the Bank of Japan, the other securities were 8.1% and 3.9% of their total assets, respectively (Bank for International Settlements, 2017, p. 72). This unprecedented "quantitative easing" by artificially increasing the demand for securities of all types (public debt, financial derivatives etc.) has significantly slowed down the devalorisation of fictitious capital.

For example, the central banks, by buying government bonds in primary or secondary markets, kept securities prices at high levels, preventing the fall of their fictitious value. But what actually do public bonds represent? Usually they do not even correspond to any material collateral. They simply represent rights to future taxes that the states will receive. Undoubtedly, preventing the decline in the value of government bonds has an economic meaning: It maintains the interest rate on sovereign debt at a low level. When the interest rate of a 100-dollar bond is 3%, and this bond is sold for 50 dollars on the secondary market, then the new 100-dollar bond that the state issues must have at least 6% interest rate to be competitive. However, as we have mentioned in Chap. 3, there is an alternative to this policy: the "haircut" of sovereign debt with social criteria and the devalorisation of its fictitious value in a controlled manner. If the central banks have to intervene so massively to "save" the value of government bonds through "quantitative easing", this is because the fiscal policies of the last decades were not sustainable.

Quantitative easing allowed the hegemonic states to borrow at a low interest rate at a time when public debt (Chart 5.2) has been growing very quickly (bank rescues, dealing with the social dimensions of the crisis etc.). However, at the same time, it slowed down the devalorisation of fictitious capital (which prevented the "haircut" of public debt, which would otherwise be inevitable) through the purchase of public bonds in primary or secondary markets.

However, monetary policy has its own limits too. The direct competition of central banks with the private sector in the government bond market has not only led to low interest rates but often to zero or even negative real interest rates: Germany, France, Spain, Italy, Japan, Norway, Sweden, Japan borrow with negative real interest rates on government bonds with various maturities (from two to ten years). According to Fitch rating agency, in June 2016, government bonds with a negative real interest rate exceeded ten trillion dollars (Orange, 2016).

The negative interest rate on sovereign debt is a severe problem, especially for organisations and funds that are legally obliged to invest a portion of their assets in government bonds, such as insurance and pension funds. It directly affects workers because it increases (often more than

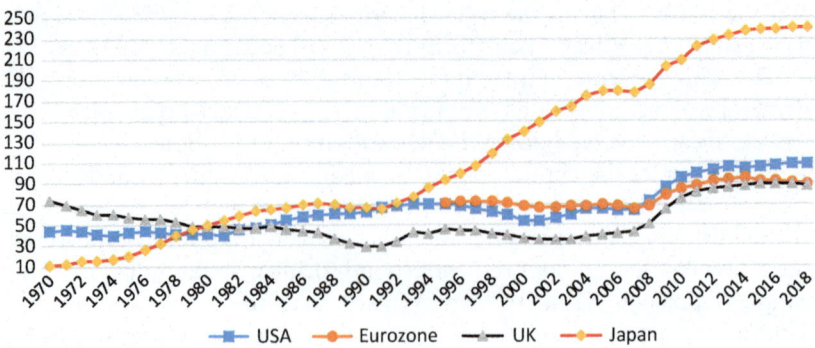

Chart 5.2   Sovereign debt in the USA, Eurozone*, UK and Japan, 1970–2018. Source: AMECO. *1975–2018

doubles) their contributions to pension funds. This is the only way for wage earners to keep hoping for a pension of 75% of their last wage.

This "quantitative easing", in other words the expansion of the money supply, took such dimensions that it led to zero or even negative real key interest rates of central banks. The real key interest rate of Fed has been in negative territory from 2008.

This situation undermines the traditional banking system, which is based on the conversion of deposits into loans, thus creating incentives to increase deposits. Instead, some European banks began to discourage deposits by treating them as a "cost". For example, a Bavarian co-operative bank, *Raiffeisenbank*, decided in 2016 to charge 0.4% on unsecured deposits over 100,000 euro to offset the cost of its own deposits in the ECB held at a 0.4% negative rate. One way or another, directly or indirectly, banks are trying to transfer to depositors the cost of their own deposits in central banks.

The banks compete with each other about which one will record the highest profits and distribute the highest dividends to their shareholders. But if the classic activity of bank intermediation, in other words the conversion of a deposit into a loan, yields less and less, then are not banks directed by monetary policy itself to increasingly risky "investments" in the various international stock markets, financial derivatives, futures, real estate and so forth? Instead of ensuring the stability of the banking system, as it should, monetary policy does exactly the opposite. In fact, it cultivates the ground for a new banking crisis. This is the reason why even the bankers themselves, such as the former chairman of *Deutsche Bank*, John Cryan, denounced the central banks' zero or negative interest rate policy. It destabilises the banking system, leading to risky speculation, Cryan said (Sims, 2017).

The ECB aligned its monetary policy to that of the Fed and the Bank of Japan with a significant delay. This inertia of the ECB made many economists believe that the dissolution of the Eurozone was almost inevitable. In July 2008, in the middle of the financial crisis, the ECB raised its nominal key interest rate to 4.5%, while the Fed reduced its own in order to moderate the forthcoming recession (Khalfa, 2014). In fact, the ECB was still worried about a possible rise in inflation, while the real risk was deflation. It was then forced to progressively reduce its key interest rate, which it, however, increased again in April and July 2011. However, the slight rise in inflation that was observed at that time was due to the rise in the prices of imported raw materials in the Eurozone, against which the key interest rate was completely impotent. Then, due to the very poor performance of the Eurozone economy, it was forced to reduce again its key interest rate, which fell to 0.25% in November 2013. The late alignment of European monetary policy to that of the Fed and the Bank of Japan had much less impact on economic activity in Europe than monetary policy could have.

From the middle of 2010 up to the beginning of 2012, with the so-called Securities Market Programme (SMP), the ECB attempted to stabilise public debt markets by buying sovereign debt on secondary markets from private banks, spending over 200 billion euros for this purpose. In December of 2011 and February of 2012, the ECB launched the Long-Term Refinancing Operations (LTRO) programme, which offered three-year loans at a very low interest rate in order to support private banks and stimulate economic activity. The result was particularly frustrating as banks have only slightly increased their loans to businesses and households. They chose to deposit the cheap money from the ECB back with the ECB despite the very low return on deposits.

The continuing tension in sovereign debt markets in the southern euro area, especially in Italy and Spain (as Greece was already out of the market), forced Mario Draghi on 26 July 2012 to make the famous announcement to do "whatever it takes" to save the euro. The Outright Monetary Transaction (OMT) programme was announced in September of the same year to make possible an unlimited purchase of sovereign debt in secondary markets.

After the major recession of 2009 (−4.4%), the Eurozone (EZ-12) showed negative growth rates in 2012 (−0.9%) and 2013 (−0.3%). It only returned to positive growth rates since 2014 (between 1.3% and 2.2%), at the same time as the ECB's monetary policy, amid internal tensions and the *Bundesbank*'s (Germany's central bank) official disagreement, was synchronised with that of other advanced economy central banks. In 2014, the ECB's nominal key interest rate, following successive reductions, reached very close to 0%, while the real interest rate on private bank deposits in the ECB turned negative.

At the same time, the ECB allocated 400 billion euros to private banks under the Targeted Long-Term Refinancing Operations (TLTRO) at an interest rate of 0.15%, provided that they would finance small- and medium-sized enterprises. Beyond this almost zero interest rate, the ECB, in order to encourage banks to lend, allowed them to convert these loans into ABSs in order to buy them back. Private banks could not only get rid of the risk of these loans, but also the tier 1 capital ratio (the ratio of a bank's core equity capital to its total risk-weighted assets required by the regulator) did not change, since financial derivatives, that is the ABSs, belong to the off-balance-sheet items.

While initially the ECB demanded the so-called sterilisation of the additional money supply generated by its purchases of sovereign debt from the banks, forcing the latter to deposit the corresponding amounts with the ECB, in 2014 it rescinded its "sterilisation demand" of the supposedly "inflationary" additional liquidity in the economy.

All of these measures, which go far beyond the mandate of the ECB, gave a new lease of life to the euro and eliminated the risk of deflation. The latter is disastrous for productive activity because enterprises are suspending their investments in anticipation of the fall in the cost of the means of production that they need, while their profit margin is reduced by the fall in the price of their own products. The rise in real interest rates resulting from deflation makes it more difficult to service public and private debt, as well as to finance business and budget deficits.

However, these measures, as already mentioned, have undesirable side effects, as they have not led to a new period of high investment and growth rates and do not cure the main problem of the economy: structural overproduction of exchange values, because supply capacity exceeds sustainable demand. Central banks deal with this structural problem as if it were a liquidity problem.

The monetary policy of central banks confronted the bubble of money capital that exploded in 2007–2008 by creating new bubbles that are about to burst again. A classic example is the real estate market that in some privileged cities and regions is experiencing a new boom, based on cheap money. The same thing happens with the shares of many companies: Since demand is higher than supply, their price is rising, while their return is decreasing, just as with government bonds.

Undoubtedly, even the central banks themselves recognise the need to return to monetary "normality". But moving from an unprecedented protracted "state of emergency" to a "state of normality" could cause new recessions. This transition requires very fine handling and "acceptable" growth rates.

Instead of analysing the various technical details of this necessary transition, we will focus on the impact that an increase in central bank key interest rates could have on sovereign debt during such a transition. If we consider the public sector, state and central banks as a single entity, the purchase of government bonds by the central bank amounts to the conversion of more or less long-term sovereign debt into very short-term debt: The central bank issues liabilities for the purchase of government bonds, which typically take the form of excess reserves held by the banks. The interest rate on these excess reserves fluctuates in line with the key interest rate of the central bank. Therefore, if the interest rate on these excess reserves rises, then the cost of financing the public debt will also increase immediately.

For instance, let us assume that the central bank ceases to buy sovereign debt and that no government bond held by the latter matures for a certain period. What will happen if the key interest rate changes within this period, for example during 2019? If the excess reserves are 50% of the sovereign debt, then a 2% increase in the interest rate on these excess reserves amounts to 1% of the sovereign debt. If the sovereign debt is 100% of GDP and if the financing cost of the sovereign debt was initially 2% of GDP, now it is 3%—amounting to an increase of 50% (Bank for International Settlements, 2017, p. 75).

The greater the volume of sovereign debt held by central banks, the greater the volume of the excess reserves held by central banks, the more difficult it is to deal with the problem of transition. The Bank of Japan, whose excess reserves are 28.5% of Japan's sovereign debt, faces the biggest problem. The Bank of England follows with excess reserves that represent 25% of UK sovereign debt, the ECB with excess reserves that are 16.6% of the Euro area sovereign debt and finally the Fed with excess reserves that represent 11.8% of US sovereign debt.

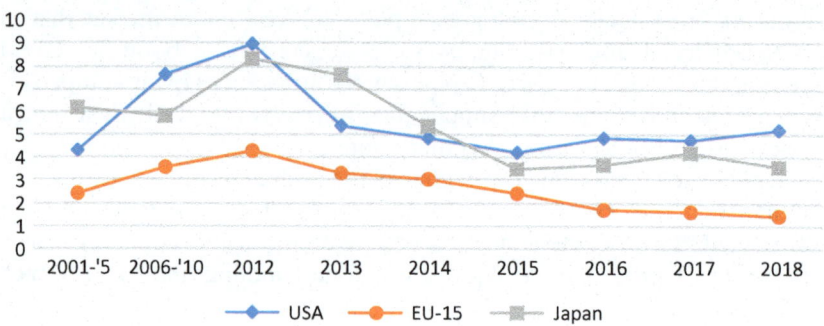

Chart 5.3 Fiscal deficit in the USA, EU-15 and Japan, 2001–2018. Source: *European Economy, Statistical Annex*, Spring 2017

Apart from the general impact on the financing cost of public debt that the phasing out of "quantitative easing" would have, monetary policy also has to face the specific problems of a transition period, the length of which depends on the average maturity time of government bonds held by central banks: 12.3 years in the UK, 8 in the USA and the Eurozone, 6.9 in Japan (Bank for International Settlements, 2017, p. 72).

Monetary policy temporarily rescued a failed financial system. However, its result was not a return to economic "normality", let us say a return to the pre-crisis rates of growth. Even the central banks themselves admit that "monetary policy cannot do everything".

The return to monetary "normality", which is now being attempted, even if it is managed in the best possible manner by central banks, will have serious consequences on productive activity. As soon as the central banks raise their key interest rate and reduce "quantitative easing", austerity policies will be reinforced. This means even lower GDP growth rates. In the EU-15 the budget deficit is already so absurdly low that there is no room for further reduction (Chart 5.3).

It is worth pointing out that GDP growth rates since 2010, although much lower than before the crisis, are largely due to US and, to a lesser extent, Japanese fiscal policy. The EU-15 benefits from the positive impact of the budget deficits of other countries on economic growth, while it applies a very restrictive budget policy, with budget deficits lower than the 3% deficit that is allowed by the Maastricht criterion. As soon as the USA and Japan reduce their budget deficits, GDP growth will decelerate further in Europe.

One has to take very seriously the concerns of the Bank for International Settlements:

> This tightening of financial conditions, together with volatility in financial markets, could have significant macroeconomic implications. [...] tighter financial conditions would depress economic activity. (Bank for International Settlements, 2017, pp. 72, 74)

BIBLIOGRAPHY

Bank for International Settlements. (2017). *87th Annual Report, 1st April 2016–31st March 2017*. Basel. Retrieved from: https://www.bis.org/publ/arpdf/ar2017e.pdf

Brenner, R. (2016). *The Economics of Global Turbulence: The Advanced Capitalist Economies from long Boom to long Downturn, 1945–2005*. London, New York: Verso.

Dossier de Presse. (2015, May 18). *L'usine du futur: Réunir la nouvelle France Industrielle*. Retrieved from: https://www.economie.gouv.fr/files/files/PDF/industrie-du-futur_dp.pdf

European Commission. (2017, Spring). *European Economy, Statistical Annex*. Retrieved from: https://ec.europa.eu/info/files/statistical-annex-european-economy-spring-2017_en

European Parliament. (2016). *Unemployment and Poverty: Greece and Other (Post-) Programme Countries*. Retrieved from: http://www.europarl.europa.eu/RegData/etudes/BRIE/2016/578991/IPOL_BRI(2016)578991_EN.pdf

Forschungsunion & AKATECH. (2013, April). *Deutschlands Zukunft als Produktionsstandort sichern. Umsetzungsempfehlungen für das Zukunftsprojekt Industrie 4.0. Abschlussbericht des Arbeitskreises Industrie 4.0*. Retrieved from: https://www.bmbf.de/files/Umsetzungsempfehlungen_Industrie4_0.pdf

Gechert, S., & Rannenberg, A. (2015). The Costs of Greece's Fiscal Consolidation. *Vierteljahrs Hefte zur Wirtschaftsforschung*, Vol. 84 (*The Greek Crisis: A Greek Tragedy?*), pp. 47–59. Retrieved from: https://doi.org/10.3790/vjh.84.3.47

Husson, M. (2013). Economie Politique du "système-euro", *Social Sciences: Trilingual Revue of Social Research*, 2–3, 163–182.

IMF. (2013, June). *Greece: Ex Post Evaluation of Exceptional Access under the 2010 Stand-By Arrangement*, IMF Country Report No. 13/156. Retrieved from: https://www.imf.org/external/pubs/ft/scr/2013/cr13156.pdf

Khalfa, P. (2014, September 11). Super Mario au secours de l'économie européenne? *Mediapart*. Retrieved from: https://blogs.mediapart.fr/pierre-khalfa/blog/110914/super-mario-au-secours-de-l-economie-europeenne

Krugman, P. (2012). *End This Depression Now!*. New York, London: W.W. Norton & Company.

OECD. (2013). *OECD Economic Surveys: Greece 2013*. Retrieved from: https://www.oecd-ilibrary.org/economics/oecd-economic-surveys-greece-2013_eco_surveys-grc-2013-en

Orange, M. (2016, August 25). Les Banquiers centraux face "la plus grande expérimentation monétaire". Retrieved from: https://www.mediapart.fr/journal/economie/250816/les-banquiers-centraux-face-la-plus-grande-experimentation-monetaire?onglet=full

Piketty T., & Saez E. (2008, March). The Evolution of Top Incomes: A Historical and International Perspective. Retrieved from: http://elsa.berkeley.edu/~saez/

Roberts, M. (2016). *The Long Depression: How it Happened, what it Happened and What Happens Next*. Chicago: Haymarket Books.

Sims, T. (2017, September, 6). Deutsche Bank demande à la BCE d'en finir avec l'argent trop facile. Retrieved from: https://fr.reuters.com/article/business-News/idFRKCN1BH16C-OFRBS

Spath, D. (Ed), Ganschar, O., Gerlach, S., Hämmerle, M., Krause, T., & Schlund, S. (2013). *Produktion Arbeit der Zukunft—Industrie 4.0*. Stuttgart: Fraunhofer Verlag.

Tombazos, S. (2011). Centrifugal Tendencies in the Euro Area. *Journal of Contemporary European Studies*, Volume 19, Issue 1, 33–46.

Tombazos, S. (2017). The Vicious Cycle of Cyprus's Economic Crisis. In Hannapi, H., Katsikides, S., & Scholz-Wäckerle, M. (Eds), *Evolutionary Political Economy in Action*: A Cyprus Symposium. Abington: Routledge.

Truth Committee on Public Debt. (2015). *Preliminary Report*, Athens: Greek Parliament. Retrieved from: https://auditoriacidada.org.br/wp-content/uploads/2014/06/Report-Greek-Truth-Committee.pdf

Varoufakis, Y. (2017). *Adults in the Room: My Battle with Europe's Deep Establishment*. New York: Vintage.

Varoufakis, Y. (2018, August 26). Greece was never bailed out—it remains locked in an EU debtor's prison. *The Guardian*. Retrieved from: https://www.theguardian.com/commentisfree/2018/aug/26/greece-was-never-bailed-out%2D%2D-it-remains-a-debtors-prison-and-the-eu-still-holds-the-keys

CHAPTER 6

Conclusion

Abstract From the early 1980s, the neoliberal policies that transformed the old Keynesian regulatory framework, transformed also the characteristics of the crises: The crisis of the 1970s was due to the fall in the profit rate. The present crisis is due to the structural slowdown in the rhythm of realisation of value. The current crisis is the crisis of the neoliberal response to the crisis of the 1970s. The neoliberal reproduction of capital survives with the support of economic policies that create new "bubbles" on the one hand, and social disasters on the other. We live in the impasse of a schema of reproduction in which money capital prevails, whose existence is only possible through severe periodic recessions, social regression and political crises.

Keywords The crisis of the 1970s and the current crisis • Realisation of value • Social reproduction • Social regression • Political hegemony

During the 1970s, the "golden" period of post-war development ended. The capital reproduction schema of Keynesian management was based on an impressive increase in labour productivity through the proliferation of Taylorist and Fordist methods in the production process. The so-called Scientific Management of Labour (as these methods are euphemistically called) was applied at a time in which the balance of power between social classes allowed the rise in the standard of living of the working class.

© The Author(s) 2019
S. Tombazos, *Global Crisis and Reproduction of Capital*, Palgrave Insights into Apocalypse Economics,
https://doi.org/10.1007/978-3-030-05725-1_6

Increasing labour productivity resulted in wage growth. At the same time, in the framework of Keynesian management, modern public health, education and transport systems, as well as pension systems, compensation for the unemployed and so forth were established. Keynesian monetary and fiscal policies had encouraged productive investment and shrunk speculation: As Keynes himself said, the "euthanasia" of speculators was pursued.

The "golden" period, however, had its dark side as well. The "Scientific Management of Labour" developed the absolute "partial worker" already described by Marx in the first volume of *Capital* and by Charlie Chaplin in his film *Modern Times*. The worker is specialised in a one and only productive movement that he repeats throughout the working day at a rhythm imposed by the supervisor, the chronometer and the mechanical systems, such as the mechanical production line. The complete separation of the intellectual work undertaken by the engineers and the manual labour undertaken by the partial worker condemns the latter to a modern version of the Sisyphus punishment.

Since the end of the 1960s, the "Scientific Management of Labour", having spread as far as it could spread from an industrial branch to another industrial branch, faced the passive and active resistance of wage labour (frequent absences from the workplace, acceleration of labour power rotation that increases the cost of managing recruitment and the cost of adapting newly recruited workers to productive requirements and practices, strikes etc.).

Capital attempted to respond to the decline in labour productivity growth, to which the crisis of the "Scientific Management of Labour" led, by replacing wage labour with constant capital. The result was to raise the organic composition of capital more than the rate of surplus value and the fall in the profit rate. Investment decelerated together with GDP growth, while unemployment rose.

During the 1970s and 1980s, some economists attributed the crisis to rising oil prices. Because mainstream economists do not have a theory of crises (it does not fit into the "general equilibrium" equations, they assume), they were looking for an exogenous factor in interpreting the crisis (Mandel, 1982). In fact, the reproduction schema or the regime of accumulation of the "golden" post-war period collapsed. From the early 1970s, the downward stage of the post-war cycle followed the upward stage.

Soon, the economic contraction led to a crisis of public finances. The state, which received less taxes (due to poor economic performance), had to manage the social consequences of the crisis (mainly mass unemployment) that required increased public expenditure.

Keynesianism had no ready answers at this conjuncture. Its success was based on both the substantial growth in labour productivity during the first stage of the post-war cycle and the efficiency of demand-supporting policies in less internationalised economies. The progressive internationalisation of national economies in the post-war era (increasing ratio of imports and exports to GDP) made demand-side policies less effective at national level: The more open an economy is, the less it benefits from demand-stimulating policies. The benefit of such policies spreads to its commercial competitors, and its impact in the country implementing them declines.

Neoliberalism, a theory for decades completely discredited and of course without any real impact on economic policy or in universities (Dixon, 2000), needed this particular historical context to step out of obscurity.

"Neoliberal policies" and "globalisation"—the same "globalisation" that, as the Bank for International Settlements recently discovered, has a catalytic impact on the balance of social power at the expense of the working class—are inextricably linked. Neoliberal policies, by deregulation of international trade, global capital movement and financial systems, have led, through "uninhibited" national and global competition, to the formation of global oligopolies and to today's globalised economy: They have thus increased the rate of exploitation of the labour force and enabled the restoration of the profit rate.

Money capital and speculative logic—the same logic that Keynes wanted to put to "euthanasia"—were integral part of the process through which the exploitation rate recovered. Travelling on a planetary scale without passports and formalities, money capital has contributed to the imposition of a productive discipline, which is seen as self-evident and necessary by the mainstream media all over the world: "To attract foreign investments a wage discipline is among other things indispensable". The coercive law of value on a global scale, the same law that creates all kinds of social regression, including ecological disaster, appears in such oversimplified discourse as the embodiment of logic.

Money capital does not take a share of the profit of the productive enterprise, thereby undermining fixed capital accumulation. In stark contrast to this, it has been a key tool in restoring industrial profit, of which, of course, it claims a great share in the form of interest and dividends.

In this process of restoring industrial profit, money capital has introduced new demands regarding the profitability of industrial capital. Through so-called corporate governance and the ease with which it withdraws from branches with low profitability to move into other branches with relatively higher profitability, at national level and world-wide, this restoration has been allowed. Productive activities that, without this corporate governance, would be considered profitable enough, are declining and disappearing, which contributes to the rising trend in the ratio Surplus Value/Accumulation.

Productive investment in new fixed capital, especially when it is techno-logically advanced, takes time to have a positive impact on productivity and relative surplus value, because it takes time to be fully integrated into the mechanical systems and the division of labour in the industrial unit. The short-term logic of money capital is imposed over the long-term logic of productive capital. This is why, today, the mechanism of relative surplus value seems to prevail less than in the post-war "golden" period, while the mecha-nism of absolute surplus value seems to be more and more decisive for the high rate of exploitation. The former is based on productivity growth that reduces the necessary working time for the reproduction of labour power (the value of labour power, not its purchasing power), while the latter is based on the prolongation of the working day and on equivalent practices such as the intensification of the working time or "flexible" part-time employment that integrates in the labour market additional labour power (Marx, 1976).

However, surplus value that is not productively invested and not pri-vately consumed by capitalists, seeks non-productive investment areas and is partly transformed into non-redeemable fictitious capital ("toxic capi-tal"): rights on future taxes through the purchase of government bonds, on future wages through loans for real estate or through consumer credit, speculation on the stock exchange, real estate, foreign exchange and so forth; in other words, excess credit of every kind that is increasingly lack-ing in collateral and investments in a "casino-economy": briefly, "colonisa-tion of the future" (Lysandrou, 2016) and "blackjack".

Fictitious capital did, however, play a decisive role in the growth rate of GDP that preceded the current structural crisis, by suppressing the symp-toms of the divergence between the rhythm of valorisation of value and the "sustainable" rhythm of realisation of value. The "bubble", accelerat-ing the rhythm of realisation, was a precondition for the moderate perfor-mance of economic activity before the crisis.

It is precisely for this reason that the neoliberal reproduction of capital survives on "technical breathing support", that is with the support of monetary policies that create new "bubbles". The monetary policy of the central banks (and mainly US fiscal policy) maintains it artificially, but without ensuring satisfactory rates of accumulation of industrial capital or GDP growth and with side effects that may soon take the form of new major crises of finance capital, that is crises of the financial system and recessions of the "real economy". The "drug" (monetary policy) has side effects, but the reduction in its dose may have far more serious and direct effects on an exhausted economy. We live in the impasse of a schema of reproduction in which money capital prevails, whose existence is only possible through periodic economic and social disasters.

The possibility of such a crisis, a crisis that does not stem from the fall in the profit rate but from the divergence between the profit rate and the rate of accumulation, is described by Marx himself in a book written more than 150 years ago:

> Taking all other circumstances as equal [i.e. the share of the profit for the private consumption of the capitalist], the amount of profit destined for transformation back into capital will depend on the amount of profit made and hence on the expansion of the reproduction process itself. But if this new accumulation comes up against difficulties of application, against a lack of spheres of investment, i.e. if branches of production are saturated and loan capital is over-supplied, this plethora of loanable money capital proves nothing more than the barriers of *capitalist* production. The resulting credit swindling demonstrates that there is no positive obstacle to the use of this excess capital. But there is an obstacle set up by its own laws of valorization, by the barriers within which capital can valorize itself as capital. (Marx, 1991, p. 639)

And, of course, this oversupplied money capital, this plethora of loan capital, "develops the need to pursue the production process beyond its capitalist barriers: too much trade, too much production, too much credit" (Marx, 1991, p. 640).

World capitalism is trapped in the same fundamental contradiction since the late 1960s: It refuses to offer what society is asking for. Social needs have grown in areas relatively incompatible with the substance of capitalism, that is, the pursuit of a high rate of profit. These social needs, in the developed world, require a new division of social working time in favour of services in the fields of education, culture, health, creative leisure management, global ecological management and so forth. These services, however, cannot be subordinated to the logic of profit without altering their meaning and content. When the public good is expropriated to become a commodity, education is downgraded to vocational training, culture to imported soap opera, health to a luxury commodity or to a privilege that can only be enjoyed by those who can pay for private insurance, leisure time to a tourist "canned product" and the ecological management of the globe to meaningless declarations.

Neoliberalism responded to the fall in the rate of profit in the 1970s by deepening this fundamental contradiction. Instead of shrinking the "space of commodity", it tried to expand it by undermining the public good and the social acquis. High profitability is no longer compatible with the satisfaction of social needs, as it was in the upward stage of the post-war cycle. Industry, where productivity can grow in leaps and bounds, is no longer creating new products comparable to the products that were the driving force behind the growth in the "golden age" of the post-war cycle, such as automobiles and household equipment.

Although microelectronics constitutes a new technological leap, its applications have affected economic activity much less than the new products of the upward stage of the cycle. On the consumption side, it is enough to compare the value of the computer to the value of the car. On the production side, with or without "robotics", the annual growth in labour productivity in the neoliberal period lags far behind its annual growth in the post-war upward stage.

We see new technologies everywhere: On the road, at home, in our pocket … everywhere except in the places where labour productivity can be augmented. It is precisely for this reason that the rise in the rate of profit could only be achieved through the decline of the wage share and the dismantlement of the social acquis. The crisis of the 1970s has never been really overcome. It was simply transformed from a crisis due to the fall in the rate of profit to a crisis due to the deceleration of the realisation process of value.

The current crisis is just the most serious episode of the same long-term downward wave that began in the 1970s. It is the "crisis" of the capitalist reaction and the neoliberal response to the crisis of the 1970s.

Never before in post-war history, perhaps in the whole of peacetime capitalist history, has there been such a long-term and at the same time general stagnation of labour productivity in the developed world as in the period 2008–2018. We are faced with a phenomenon of conflict between productive relations and productive forces, as Marx would probably have said.

The law of value allows us to understand this conflict, but it does not automatically and mechanically lead to its overcoming. Capital and its institutions show no intention of changing orientation. They deviate from neoliberal orthodoxy on many levels (monetary policy, rescue of the banking system with public money etc.) and as much as needed to ensure the persistence of the same neoliberal ideology that cannot imagine any other economic or social horizon than that of the commodity logic and its fetishism, of which it reveals the "primitive instincts": the anti-social excesses and the general disregard for the environment to which this commodity logic leads.

The preservation of the system is ensured through social regression. In this historical context, it is also no coincidence that the democratic acquis is dismantled: often in the name of "counter-terrorism policy" and always in favour of bureaucratic and authoritarian political management. Thus, the very values of modern civilisation itself are undermined and the door is opened to far-right extremism of all sorts.

The social disaster and the parody of parliamentary democracy in Greece since 2010 may not be the exception to the rule but the beginning of a new capitalist "normality". Such "normality", however, belongs to a dense historical time, to a perpetual crisis of "social reproduction" and "political hegemony" (Ioakeimoglou, 2017) with an open outcome whose first indications in the USA and Europe are already obvious.

BIBLIOGRAPHY

Dixon, K. (2000). *Die Evangelisten des Marktes: Die britischen Intellektuellen und der Thatcherismus*. Konstanz: UVK-Uni-Verlag.

Ioakeimoglou, E. (2017). Crisis of Capitalism, Crisis of Social Reproduction: And after that? *Kokkino*, 9 [in Greek].

Mandel, E. (1982). *La crise 1974–1982: les faits, leur interprétation marxiste*. Paris: Flammarion.

Marx, K. (1976). *Capital: A Critique of Political Economy*. Volume One. London, New York: Penguin Books.

Marx, K. (1991). *Capital: A Critique of Political Economy*. Volume Three. London, New York: Penguin Books.

Lysandrou, P. (2016). Colonisation of the Future: An alternative view of financialization and its portents. *Journal of Post Keynesian Economics*, Volume 39, Issue 4, 444–472.

Index[1]

[1] Note: Page numbers followed by 'n' refer to notes.

© The Author(s) 2019
S. Tombazos, *Global Crisis and Reproduction of Capital*, Palgrave
Insights into Apocalypse Economics,
https://doi.org/10.1007/978-3-030-05725-1

Printed by Printforce, the Netherlands